BRILLIANT BREAKTHROUGHS
FOR THE SMALL BUSINESS OWNER:

Fresh Perspectives on Profitability,
People, Productivity, and Finding
Peace in Your Business

Volume 4

Compiled by
Maggie Mongan

Brilliant Breakthroughs, Inc.
Milwaukee, WI

ENDORSEMENTS

This edition of *Brilliant Breakthroughs for the Small Business Owner* raises the bar on the 4 Performance Pillars winning formula for small business success. Each author distills years of quintessential experience into applicable and measurable operational strategies for small business performance. As I assess the relaunch of my post COVID-19 business strategy in the coming year, it is reassuring to know I have access to an authentic and cutting-edge group of small business owners who openly share their models for success, and who are ready to support beyond the pages of the book. The Brilliant Breakthroughs' online platform, podcast, and small business summit is my go-to forum for inspiration, small business innovation, and practical information.

— **Dr. Ellema Albert Neal,** Ed.D, BS
Author & Small Business Owner

Brilliant Breakthroughs for the Small Business Owner is a must-read for any small business owner or entrepreneur. I found the chapter on imposter syndrome especially poignant. The author turns the phrase, "fake it until you make it" into "faith until you become it" as he describes *The 4 Secrets to Overcoming Imposter Syndrome*™. These insights gave me the clarity and tools I needed to navigate my own nagging imposter syndrome. The stories that are woven in really brought the concepts to life and made this a joy to read.

— **Cindy Strom**, BSN, RN,
Certified High Performance Coach
Owner High Performance Living LLC

Brilliant Breakthrough for the Small Business Owner provides key tools to help you achieve success with more freedom and peace of mind. It delivers ideas to increase profitability and productivity more healthily. By implementing the tips, this book is going to help your business and your life will go to the next level.

— **Dr. Isabel Pérez,** Ph.D.
Co-founder of ISAMIZU, Global Conscious Wellness

Being a business owner comes with many obstacles. When you're doing the work and setting yourself up for success, it can be challenging to see your own blind zones.

Brilliant Breakthroughs for the Small Business Owner is an insightful and powerful collection of tools to help you see areas you may be missing within your business structure, in order to set yourself up for success. This is a definite must-read for any business owner ready for abundance, success, and to change the conversation around money in a fun and energetic way.

— **Katrina Potter**
Entrepreneur, Wellness Coach, and Business Owner

This book is an exceptional resource for any professional, especially business owners, looking to develop your own perspective on success. I really enjoyed the focus on celebrating people through emphasizing culture and communication throughout the organization. It also provides a critical guide on how to start having the right conversations with the right people at the right times - truly a unique focus that contributes to high-performing teams. A must-read to evolve your business into the culture-driven HUMAN organization of the future.

— **Aaron M. Rindt**
Manager, Community, Culture & Employee Engagement,
ETE Reman

During these times of far-reaching civil and public health challenges, here is a book that brings fresh thinking to how one might observe and make meaningful progress, professional as well as personal. Highly recommended.

— Michael Carter
Founder and CEO, Intercultural Competence Edge

I highly recommend *Brilliant Breakthroughs for the Small Business Owner* for the not-for-profit community, especially those involved in religious work, as they tend to run their information flow with spit, rubber bands, and chewing gum. In other words, they follow the isolated process.

— Kirk Gliebe, Rabbi and Director
Devar Emet Messianic Synagogue & Outreach

This book is an insightful and delightful read. I love how well each author "dialed it down" in terms that easily are understood and applied. A priceless collection of experiential guidance, tools, and practices to help you achieve success and fulfillment in business and ALL aspects of life.

— Martha Childress, Publisher/Radio Host
The Natural Choice Network

Once again, Maggie scores a touchdown as she explores the concept of personal values in relationship to profitability. In this chapter, the concept of identifying and utilizing core values is seamlessly linked with success and profitability. Since values are abstract and only reveal themselves through action and behavior, the concepts Maggie brings to light become concrete and develop into marketable resources. Many small business owners get so wrapped up in the day to day operations of leading and managing the business end of their enterprise, they minimize the significance of who they are and how they show up in the world as their biggest asset leading to profitability. A small business owner's values are as much of a company's inventory as the product he or she sells to make a profit. It can be a challenging concept to look at congruency between these two aspects of core values and making money. It is also an intriguing concept to think of having FREE resources that are being under-utilized when it comes to small business profitability. If you want to learn more about the ways core values reveal themselves in terms of profitability - this chapter is a must-read!

— **Susan White,** LCSW
Lifeskills Center, Ltd.

This book is a wonderful read for any business owner just getting started or feeling overwhelmed. Business owners can benefit from a new awareness of four key areas of profitability, people, productivity, and peacefulness. The application of the concepts found in this book offers peace of mind in a fast-paced world.

— **Dr. Carla Burns, PHD**
Author, Speaker, Quantum Success Coach,
CEO-QiVibe Digital HealthApp

Today's entrepreneurs are looking for the Swiss Army knife to get back more time while scaling their business. *Brilliant Breakthroughs for the Small Business Owner* is that Swiss Army knife. It provides valuable insights and strategies from hands-on business experts that will help today's entrepreneurs thrive in the new business economy.

— **Tony Jalan**
Certified Business Growth and Marketing Advisor

As an entrepreneur, I learned everything the hard way. On the job, baptism by fire, if you will. I learned early on, that if you step into a new opportunity and don't know how to do it, learn it quickly, then surround yourself with people who know more than you do. Most importantly, no matter what life throws at you, get back up. With this book series, *Brilliant Breakthroughs for the Small Business Owner*, you have just that. An opportunity to learn from other experts on profitability, people, productivity, and peace. You will learn what to do, and even more important, what not to do.

— George A. Santino
Speaker and Author of
Get Back Up: From the Streets to Microsoft Suites

In a world where you are required to be fast-moving, dynamic, and agile — this book provides actionable items that can make any small business exceptional. As a small business owner, myself, this read was extremely timely with ways that people can become a better leader, have the right conversations with your people, and transform your strategies that elevate your business. Take time for yourself and read this book so you can further lead your business into the future.

— Zech Dahms
Culture Architect — Perennial Culture

In the book, *Brilliant Breakthroughs for the Small Business Owner*, Dennis' chapter provides a great foundational knowledge (history) that relates to why we are in the 4th Industrial Revolution and the importance of the small business' ability to be agile, innovative, and adaptive. Dr. Hill simplifies the complexity of the era and the businesses of the future into simple, fundamental examples of how to survive today and tomorrow. A ***MUST READ*** for the entrepreneurs of the gig economy.

— Nov Omana, HRIP
CEO/Founder, Collective HR Solutions, Inc.

The perfect book to running a business, rather than having the business run you. If you're a business owner and wonder how the big companies got to where they are, Jyun Shimizu will point you in the right direction. Your business may be small in size, but you've got to think big, and this book will show you the ins and logical sequence of time tested methods that will take you from dreamer to reality and beyond.

— Steven E. Schmitt
Bestsellerguru.com, Publisher and Author

America is at a national inflection point – Social justice and climate change need to be addressed in an integrated way. Environmental justice is only possible when societal injustices and inequity are solved along through policies and approaches that provide clean, affordable energy and improved air quality to everyone. What I find compelling about Compassionate Diversity® is that it creates a canvas that's essential for envisioning a clean energy future. No one is excluded. Because it's through leveraging differences that we solve the world's most pressing problems.

— Lisa Horuczi Markus
Energy Equity Advocate, Management Consultant
and author of the FPA-recommended book
Living a Blessed Life: Walking in Faith, Growing in Wealth

Dennis's recognition that data is a golden asset and should be leveraged for growth is powerful. This is so often overlooked, and he provides actionable ways to make it a gold mine in your business.

— Candace Spears
Founder & CEO, Spears Sparrow Collective

This book is chucked with a plethora of wisdom from the *Brilliant Practicing Experts*™. The four performance pillars are the foundation for business owners and each author focuses their expertise to support a pillar. Between the book, podcast, online summit, and mobile app, the authors continue to give insights to support and help you grow your business. Melinda and Ryan Van Fleet capture this beautifully with their chapter on confidence. They explain why every business must have confidence rooted in their core to thrive in their business. That's just one nugget, read the book, there is so much more inside.

— Nancy Schwab
#1 Bestselling Author,
The App Mama and Founder at Unleashed Mobile Apps

In the book, *Brilliant Breakthroughs for the Small Business Owner*, Shalini provides accessible and actionable methods for optimizing culture to drive business results. Her human approach shows how leaders can inspire their people through change and uncertainty to achieve positive business results. *Flip the Paradigm* is an indispensable read for any small business leader striving for success in 2020 and beyond.

— Lisa Whiteman, CEBS, MBA
Employee Benefits Expert, Willis Towers Watson

You hold in your hands, *Brilliant Breakthroughs for the Small Business Owner*. It is a perfect storm of examples and applications for today's entrepreneurs. Dr. Jyun Shimizu will help you with a five-step plan to unlock the best version of yourself, discover the mindset patterns that are helping or hurting you in life and business. And, with his *Your Quantum Nature*™, you will understand your current perspective and then make the changes to unlock a new, more abundant perspective in your business and personal life. Every business owner, small or large, could learn from a fresh perspective and the ability to find peace of mind in your business.

— Patrick K. Porter, Ph.D.
The inventor of the World's First Portable, Light & Sound Device, and Founder BrainTap® Technology

As an entrepreneur, I can totally relate to Mike's chapter. I used to think I wasn't good enough or knowledgeable enough and had the same money related problems as Mike did. It wasn't until I read his chapter that I realized a shift I made, that had everything to do with releasing fear, completely changed my outcome. Mike's chapter is a perfect read for entrepreneurs and small business owners who are struggling with money. Maybe you don't realize that you have Impostor Syndrome. I didn't!

— Stacy Kaat
Photographer, Creator of the online course "The Entrepreneurs Blueprint to Personal Branding for Profit," Personal Brand Coach, & #1 Bestselling Business Book Author

This book is both insightful and timely. Just as technology has continued to be the 'great disruptor', it has become the 'great connector' during COVID. As we ponder what life will be after COVID (or A.D. "After Disruption"), the fourth industrial revolution will play a key transformational role in how we work, live, and play. This book inspires the thinking that conceives, creates, and builds small businesses, and can grow and transform mid and large businesses.

— Patricia A. Ippoliti, Ph.D., MBA
President, PI Associates, LLC
Lecturer and Lead Faculty, Columbia University

Entrepreneurship is like walking the high wire without a net — on a regular basis. It requires unwavering confidence in yourself and your vision.

In their chapter: *Building Confidence Along with a Successful Business – From the Ground Up*, Melinda and Ryan Van Fleet share their best tips to help *you* successfully navigate the rough seas of entrepreneurial life. Melinda and Ryan faced enormous obstacles on their way to building multiple successful businesses. Having arrived, now they're passionate about sharing their blueprint to success with others.

Each, in their own way, role model and teach: confidently staying the course through rough waters, knowing you have what it takes to successfully come out the other side. I can think of no one better to help budding entrepreneurs get off to a great start on their journey than two such time-tested successful entrepreneurs.

Whether you're just considering entrepreneurship, or have already begun, get this book today!

— Debbra Lupien
International Best Selling Author of
Akasha Unleashed - The Missing Manual to You

When we interview, negotiate terms, present our products, we are selling ourselves first and then our products or services. *Brilliant Breakthroughs for the Small Business Owner* shares simple, tangible ways to align our mind, body, and spirit to maximize our well-being and increase our business success in every way. A must-read for anyone who wants to gain more peace and profits!

— Melissa Soete
Vice President of Business Development,
Color Street

If your culture and team are struggling and you have no idea how to fix it the insights in *Brilliant Breakthroughs for the Small Business Owner* will help your small business compete for "Best Places to Work." Learn how to take your underproductive employees and create a culture that out-performs and increases your bottom line.

With the current pandemic, we as small business owners have the opportunity to give our businesses a fresh perspective. The *Brilliant Breakthroughs* book is a must-read for those who want to innovate their business.

— Cheryl Litvin
First Associated Insurance Agencies Inc.
Insurance Agent, and OSHA Outreach Trainer

Choosing the entrepreneurial path is not an easy feat. That's why I'm always on the lookout for valuable resources to continue to grow my business. I'm glad I found this book! *Brilliant Breakthroughs for the Small Business Owner* is filled with inspiring stories written by real entrepreneurs who are out there pursuing their true passion. I particularly enjoyed the chapter about confidence because I believe that confidence is essential not only to start a business but to grow a business in an environment that is never certain. So, if you would like a great dose of inspiration, this book is for you!

— Cloris Kylie, MBA
Best-selling author of *Beyond Influencer Marketing*

If you want to be successful in your business and life, there is an easy and quick way. It's to know how to use our consciousness and vibration. Dr. Jyun Shimizu is such a kind and positive person. It makes so much sense why he is so successful. His book will not only help business owners succeed but also everyone who wants to live healthy and happy.

— Michiko Hayashi
Ambassador and Global Director,
Non-profit organization Emoto Peace Project

This book belongs in every small business owner's "survive and thrive" tool kit. Each chapter provides relevant and wise guidance; taken as a whole, the book is an inspiration. *Brilliant Breakthroughs for the Small Business Owner, Vol. 4*, helps every reader establish peace and success in their business, even in these turbulent times.

— Kimberly Hand
Creator of Kimmunitee, LLC

BRILLIANT BREAKTHROUGHS
FOR THE SMALL BUSINESS OWNER:

*Fresh Perspectives on Profitability,
People, Productivity, and Finding
Peace in Your Business*

Volume 4

**Compiled by
Maggie Mongan**

**Brilliant Breakthroughs, Inc.
Milwaukee, WI**

BRILLIANT BREAKTHROUGHS FOR THE SMALL BUSINESS OWNER:
Fresh Perspectives on Profitability, People, Productivity,
and Finding Peace in Your Business - Volume 4

Paperback ISBN: 978-0-9994375-7-5
Hardcover ISBN: 978-0-9994375-9-9
EBook ISBN: 978-0-9994375-8-2

Library of Congress: 2018912690

First Published in the USA in 2020 by Brilliant Breakthroughs, Inc.
Publishing Advisor: Spotlight Publishing™

Book Cover: Maggie Mongan with Angie Analya
Interior Design: Soumi Goswami
Group Photograph:
Collaboration between Stacy Kaat Photography & Wilmot Designs

For Information Contact:
Brilliant Breakthroughs, Inc.
www.BrilliantBreakthroughs.com

DEDICATION

This book is dedicated to Small Business Owners.
You are our economy's accelerant.

CONTENTS

PERFORMANCE PILLAR 1: PROFITABILITY

PERFORMANCE PILLAR 2: PEOPLE

PERFORMANCE PILLAR 3: PRODUCTIVITY

ACKNOWLEDGEMENTS

To my beloved Chris, who is the steady of my world. He generously gives up his time with me so I can do what I must to produce this book, weekly podcast, mobile app, and virtual summit. I couldn't be progressing through my recovery and managing everything else, without his patience, support, and tender loving care. Together we appreciate the daytime warmth, moonlight evenings, and even rain showers.

There are many people to thank for co-creating this extraordinary book. Thank you, beloved 2020 contributing author team, for delivering high-quality chapter content and making this accomplishment one to remember. Big hugs to The Community of Brilliant Practicing Experts™, who have traveled with us this past year. Without you, this would have been more difficult to accomplish. Your wisdom and actions are appreciated!

Special thanks to Nancy Lucchesi Schwab for an excellent mobile app: **BrilliantBizBook** to serve Small Businesses. Theresa Wilmot for supporting our graphic needs and making us shine brilliantly. Stacy Kaat for making our headshots look stellar! Lori Bonaparte for a splendid chapter Introduction.

Additional gratitude to our Advising Publisher, Becky Norwood of Spotlight Publishing. Becky is a consummate professional and wise guide. Her impeccable guidance makes publishing a breeze!

There's far too many teachers, mentors, colleagues, and friends to mention this time! I acknowledged many of you in Volume 1 of this series. Many of you, who hold a special place in my heart. We always welcome each of you to our table.

INTRODUCTION

THE BRILLIANT QUESTION:

Maggie, why are you writing a book?

When speaking with George A. Santino, a retired Microsoft Partner, and Serial Entrepreneur, he stated, "The American Dream is alive and well. You can start at the bottom and work hard. If you do, anything is achievable."[1] I wholeheartedly agree with George, who is the personification of The American Dream.

THE BRILLIANT ANSWER:

Contemporary business requires small business owners to think and act differently than they did in the 20th century. Small businesses of the 21st century must find the balancing act between traditional business basics and unconventional techniques. This isn't as easy as it appears. There is a noticeable disconnect between the support system (trainers, coaches, mentors, etc.) for small businesses and what small business owners need to survive and thrive.

This book shares fresh perspectives on profitability, people, productivity, and peacefulness, for you to experiment with by applying them to your business. Our goal is to support small business owners in finding their potential solutions to develop their winning formula for business success.

THE BRILLIANT REASON:

The American Dream is a viable reality in this century. It provides equal opportunity for all who pursue their dream. Those who create the right actions, which are spurred from the right thoughts, will reap the rewards.

Many people will start a business. Most are wantrepreneurs (those who talk about business ownership but don't do the work to build and deliver a successful business). This book is created for those who are seriously committed to doing the work and gaining prosperity. Ready for the good news? You can stop banging your head against the wall and quit working all hours of the night. This book is filled with all sorts of fresh perspectives for you to experiment with to find your personal secret to success.

In *The Entrepreneur's Solution*, Mel Abraham wrote, "This country was built on principles of entrepreneurialism, equity, self-determination, and opportunity. Fulfilling our potential, as individuals and as a nation is simply a matter then of reawakening that innate spirit."[2] The American Dream evolved through settlers, who became entrepreneurs and small business owners. These early founders of The American Dream started their businesses out of necessity. Some thrived to build great businesses, while others dwindled. All had the entrepreneurial spirit. Those who excelled learned how to master small business success.

Let's fast-forward to this century. If you are a seriously committed and growth-focused Small Business Owner, we know you're seeking new ways to:

- become more profitable
- develop better quality working relationships with your team and others
- explore and experiment with new productivity practices and tools
- find more peace within your business.

Why? For you to build a profitable business and experience a more joyful and fulfilling life. We get it, and you do too! We wrote this book to share some of our best practices and unconventional techniques to successfully grow YOUR Business. It's amazing what comes out of the mouths of Practicing Experts when they are sharing their wisdom.

The 21st century requires Small Business Owners (SBOs) to think and work differently to gain wins. When you are playing a new board game, you usually read the rules of the game, don't you?

Sure you do. Why? You want to assure you improve your probability of winning. Business is the same. There are basic rules for all businesses. We know these rules support strong business.

What's the difference in the rules for small business success between the last and this century? The internet and technological advancement. Good, bad, or indifferent, the internet has both helped and hindered small business success.

The internet has created endless opportunities for SBOs to share their offerings with the world. Conversely, the internet is filled with a plethora of information – useful, accurate, and inaccurate. In a short period of time, humankind has become gluttons of information.

Even with technological advancements, many business basics are still required. In the 21st century, businesses still needs marketing, sales, customers, systems, accounting, etc., for business operations to run effectively and efficiently. Technology adds another layer of simplicity and complexity to any small business operation.

Technology provides opportunities for:

- greater reach to expand a business' marketplace
- around-the-clock promotion via social media and online advertising
- more information to consume efficiencies

- perpetual distractions via *Bright Shiny Objects* popping up
- more Experts and UN-Experts are vying for your attention and money.

A new learning curve and balancing act for this century's SBO is far different than the last century. It is a necessity for small businesses to swiftly secure success. Today's SBOs are required to immediately work with experts to shave years off their learning curve to secure their position in the marketplace. When SBOs take consistent actions to secure profitability, they move beyond surviving.

Today's wide-reaching arm of the internet introduces you to an infinite number of service providers to help you grow your business.

Warning: All providers are not created equally.

There are plenty of experts in the marketplace. Experts are experienced and knowledgeable in a particular topic. Experts are masterful because they are practiced in their expertise or focused specialty.

Today's SBO has plenty of experts and UN-experts approaching them. The UN-experts are in strong force and you've probably engaged with them – vowing to never again. The UN-expert is usually an expert at online marketing, but not an expert at whatever it is they're offering. They promote well and engage you enough to secure your purchase. Unfortunately, their expertise stops there. They don't deliver at an expert level whatever the topic is you bought. The UN-expert tends to keep its customers in a state of mediocrity or perpetual need for their services.

Good news! You don't have to settle for UN-experts. In fact, a group of us believes SBOs deserve much better than what the marketplace is commonly providing for support. Over the past five years, I have been selecting and vetting Practicing Experts. There are many Practicing Experts in the marketplace. Those who are willing to openly share how they blend their best practices and unconventional techniques to build winning strategies and practical tactics to amplify their business success are collaborating authors of this book.

Some of you may ask, "How do you know they're practicing experts, Maggie?" For almost a decade, I had the honor of being trained to be one of the industry's top performers, as an Executive Recruiter and Certified Senior Account Manager specializing in placing Change Agents into organizations. Additionally, I've coached executives, SBOs, non-profit leaders, and other professionals for 20+ years. Last, I've been coaching SBOs for 15+ years.

In the late 1990s, I started saying to all the Change Agents I was recruiting, "It's all about being an Agent of Change; not an Agent for Change." Over the years, I've refined this to, *"Don't be an agent for change; be the agent OF change."* As you can see, I am an advocate for appropriate change. How successful business was conducted in the 1990s and even 2000s isn't enough for today's small business. Change - appropriate change, is required for SBOs to succeed in business. Most SBOs already know this, but they are unsure what to do about it.

This perplexed me too! For the past seven years, I've been seeking a solution. What is it you ask? You're reading it. I invited other experts to build a collaborative *Community of Brilliant Practicing Experts*™ to bring proven and effective fresh perspectives to Small Business Owners. To reveal our commitment level to you, we created a free mobile app named **BrilliantBizBook** to support the readers of our book series. This book is the fourth volume in the #1 Bestselling Annual Business Book Series for Small Business, designed to continue giving you different fresh perspectives to experiment with throughout the years.

All this has me singing the lyrics to the original *Ghostbusters* movie, "Who ya gonna call?" Hopefully, your answer isn't the slick marketers who will be ghosted next year. Rather, it's to engage with Brilliant Practicing Experts™ once you read their chapter. Why? This is how you will learn this century's winning formula of success.

Tip: Most, not all, UN-experts keep you in a state of mediocre busy-ness work. Why? When you only gain mediocre results, you still need them and will pay them more money to get additional mediocre results. Even though they say otherwise, many UN-experts want you to become only moderately successful.

I know, their behavior is not acceptable! Since we are a society that is addicted to being busy, this has become a perfect storm for many online marketers. Unfortunately, they are capitalizing on this and robbing you of your profitability, productivity, and finding peace in your business.

What's a better approach to 21st century small business success? Blending Best Practices and technology to create unconventional approaches. Why? Guided by a *Brilliant Practicing Expert*™, this approach will provide you and your business with unconventional results. *Brilliant Practicing Experts*™ focus on attracting customers (catch), teach you what you need to learn so you can do it independently from them (feed), then, encourages you to experiment with your new teachings (release), and are available if you need assistance (support).

Remember: Some information on the internet is accurate and some is inaccurate. If it was about having access to information, wouldn't we all be rich, physically fit, and beautiful by now?

Clue: For the first time in history, we are currently experiencing an information surplus and a deficit of application.

Your business's success is dependent upon you (1) securing the appropriate information, and (2) learning how to appropriately apply it to your business's circumstances.

Today's SBO has a variety of options available on what to offer and a myriad of delivery alternatives. Some techniques better support certain types of expertise or customers. There is a plethora of success options to consider; yet, some might not support your business as well as others.

How do you learn which approach is best? Experiment. The United States of America was founded by immigrants who learned how to support themselves through entrepreneurial activities and developing small businesses. Those who practiced until they succeeded, built a growing business. Eventually, some of them became founding businesses of America. These early founders of The American Dream understood the value of experimenting.

Everything was new to these early business experimenters. The Founders of American business needed to swiftly try new approaches and learn which ones did or didn't deliver favorable gains. Those who found success strategies and techniques became prosperous. Those who didn't find business success may not have survived.

The 21st century may not have mortality attached to business success for most, as it did in the 16th and 17th centuries, but it still requires an unwavering commitment from the SBO. The commitment is one of first surviving and then thriving. This requires and invites SBOs to endless exploring and experimenting to find favorable results for their business. Those who persistently take action win. Those who take action on the right things win BIG.

Gary Vaynerchuk, high profile American Serial Entrepreneur often referred to as GaryVee, is known by his followers for advocating action. He frequently references hustling. Often, you hear him say things like, "Work, that's how you get it", "Stop crying; keep hustling", or "Without hustle, talent will only carry you so far".

Vaynerchuk is a proponent of taking action and experimentation to shorten an entrepreneur's learning curves.

On a July 7, 2017 Instagram Live, GaryVee said, "Entrepreneurship emerges as culture."[3] The culture, he elaborated about is one of action. He encouraged wantrepreneurs to be practical and appropriately prepare for their business by gaining tutelage before and during entrepreneurship. He also emphasized a business's success rate is improved through experimentation – just like the early founders of The American Dream.

Typically, the right thoughts and right actions deliver favorable results. Some, not all, of the Best Practices of corporations are favorable for small business success. Conversely, there are many strategies, techniques, mindsets, and behaviors that would become unfavorable if scaled to larger organizations.

I still notice many former corporate employees, who were downsized during this century's Great Recession, have become Small Business Owners. They're either trying to behave *corporate* in a small business setting or act as if they are hyperallergic to anything which *feels* it came from their former corporate setting. I encourage former corporate folks to quit sabotaging themselves and fully step into small business ownership with a clean slate to improve their business's success rate.

Caution: Similar to corporate settings, the behaviors which secured your promotion aren't the same actions and behaviors that will help you break into the next level of success – there are different game plans for each level. The rules change when you change levels. The game is played differently to excel on each new level. Small business success doesn't promote its business owners. Instead, it secures scalability or another level of expansion for the business.

Each new level has its own rules for you to successfully master.

NOW, WHAT?

Are you a committed Small Business Owner who seeks ways to make your small business more profitable and peace-filled so you can further step into living your potential? If so, you are going to enjoy this book. Figure 1 is a *COVID-19 style* photo of our 2020 Brilliant Practicing Experts™ Author Team.

Figure 1.

Brilliant Practicing Experts™ 2020 Team of "Brilliant Breakthroughs for the Small Business Owner: Fresh Perspectives on Profitability, People, Productivity, and Finding Peace in Your Business (Vol 4)".

This extra-ordinary team has created this book (Volume 4) for you to explore and experiment with fresh perspectives to improve your business's performance.

We have organized our chapter topics into **The 4 Performance Pillars for Small Business Success™** model: Profitability, People,

Brilliant Breakthroughs, Inc. Collaborative Image
by Stacy Kaat Photography & Wilmot Designs

Productivity, and Peacefulness. Over the past 2 decades of serving businesses, I've noticed all business activities can be categorized into these 4 categories or Performance Pillars. The size and industry of a business doesn't alter this model.

When you review **The 4 Performance Pillars for Small Business Success™** model (see Figure 2), you will see The 4 Performance Pillars in the center. I have added two columns for you to discern where you or your business may need to strengthen a Performance Pillar.

Figure 2.

THE 4 PERFORMANCE PILLARS FOR SMALL BUSINESS SUCCESS™

The column on the left, *Experience this when I DON'T have it* column gives you keywords to assess if you are lacking (or not). The column on the right, *Experience this when I DO have it* column

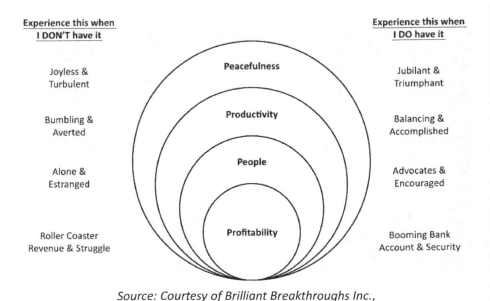

Source: *Courtesy of Brilliant Breakthroughs Inc.,*
https://brilliantbreakthroughs.com/

reveals if you have been working these areas of your business effectively. The key is to fortify each of these 4 Performance Pillars.

The following is a brief description of each of the 4 Performance Pillars.

Performance Pillar 1: Profitability

The primary determinant of Business Success is if your business is profitable. We train on these topics: financials, product development, sales, marketing, branding, operations, business models, your business's purpose-vision-mission for alignment, and anything related to profit.

Performance Pillar 2: People

People are what makes the world go around – and your business too. We train on these topics: effective networking, social media, team development, employees, your business's ideal customer, business allies (joint ventures, etc., customers, and anything related to relationship building and people.

Performance Pillar 3: Productivity

Productivity practices can make or break a business. Simplifying your activities may be easier than what you're making it out to be. We train on these topics: time management (which really doesn't exist, simplifying techniques, automated systems, tech and apps to support us being more effective and efficient, and anything related to productivity.

Performance Pillar 4: Peacefulness

Peacefulness is a possibility when you have a mindful and profitable business. It isn't necessary to polarize peace and profit. Peace is one of the elusive elements of Business Success that doesn't need to be far-fetched. We train on these topics: self-management, balanced leadership, and self-leadership, utilizing core values, daily practices, mindset, overall well-being, and anything related to peaceful prosperity.

Note: The 4 Performance Pillars for Small Business Success™ model is one of the Small Business' Evolution. It illustrates how Profitability anchors your business. Profit is always at the forefront. Since people decide whether to make a purchase or not, People are the next essential ring surrounding Profit.

There are many moving parts that need attention while conducting business. Learning how to be effective and efficient is essential; thus, Productivity is the next ring after People. The more people involved; the more Productivity becomes a focus. People don't want to, nor should they, work in an unpeaceful workplace. Peace is the outer ring, which encapsulates all the other activities.

At first glance, many SBOs will see this as I described. At another glance, SBOs may say the sequence could be reversed. This is the beauty of this model. Depending on your current business performance focus, you could move any one of the 4 pillars around since each pillar integrates with all the others.

Hint: I do suggest you work the model as described because you can have all the peace you'd like to have, but if you don't have profit, your peace and business won't be lasting too long.

It's our intention to help you explore fresh perspectives in each *of* **The 4 Performance Pillars for Small Business Success™** to have brilliant breakthroughs for yourself, as well as your business' performance.

WHAT'S NEXT?

Before our *Brilliant Practicing Experts*™ bring you the WOW! in each of their chapters, please take a moment to learn how the book is designed for you to use as a guide. Also, please engage with us on our mobile app: **BrilliantBizBook**. You may be surprised by what we have there. Have some fun experimenting and shining brightly!

Brilliant Breakthroughs for the Small Business Owner

HOW TO USE THIS BOOK:

This book is a compilation or anthology of 9 authors, who are *Brilliant Practicing Experts™*, willing to share their wisdom and winning formulas with you, the small business owner.

As you read the book, you may notice it feels as if you are reading 9 different books. Why? Each chapter was written by a different author. Out of respect to each author who has already created their customer base and a communication style within their marketplace, we honored their unique communication style throughout their chapter. We prefer this approach because we want you to know exactly what to expect when you reach out to engage with each of our authors.

This book is designed to introduce and wisdom-share fresh perspectives, so you may create some brilliant breakthroughs for yourself and your business's performance.

Use this book as a guide over the next year. Whatever you do, please don't only read this book and put it on the shelf! Instead, we invite you to experiment with the new ideas presented here. Learn and apply, practice, and tweak, and then when you have a new best practice, smile, and share your good news with us!

What you won't find in this book are advertisements. No one will be pitching their products or services to you. Our goal is to wisdom-share fresh perspectives for small business success.

BOOK LAYOUT:

This book's layout is organized via **The 4 Performance Pillars for Small Business Success™** described in the Introduction.

PERFORMANCE PILLAR 1: PROFITABILITY

Chapter 1:
The Financial Freedom Trail
by Anne Mank, CFP, CPA

Sometimes when you are a small business owner, it feels like you are walking in the wilderness. You see the summit ahead of you, but you are lost in the woods. Many times, it is the stories we tell ourselves which stop us from our financial goals. Follow the journey of Annie as she makes her first climb up The Financial Freedom Trail and learn how having the right tools, plan, and guide will help you reach the top of the mountain successfully. You will be able to start building your own *Financial Freedom Survival Kit*™ and know how to handle your cash once it starts to flow into the business with *The Cashflowing Model*™. Being a small business owner is no walk in the park, but it can be the most exciting adventure of your life.

Chapter 2:
Uplevel Your Business by Replacing Your Irreplaceable Employees: Move to Indispensable Key Talent for Ultimate Success
by Mark Boeder

All businesses claim they want to grow their business with top talent; yet, most businesses still use the antiquated *just-in-time* recruitment process. A hiring manager, with a position opening, enrolls Human Resources to post the position and canvas the market to see who might be seeking a new job. This typical *Post and Pray* approach rarely results in finding great candidates.

The better approach is to support your success by learning how to attract *Indispensable Key Talent by* developing *The Indispensable Key Talent Search Team*™ for your company. When you do this, you will create a team of high impact employees, who will become the game changers you need to succeed short- and long-term. Your company's competitive advantage is your people. Companies have to build a plan to connect with high impact *Indispensable Key Talent* as part of succession planning. Now is the time to effectively and efficiently uplevel your success and grow exponentially.

PERFORMANCE PILLAR 2: PEOPLE

Chapter 3:
The Hidden Cost of Doing Business
by Susan McCuistion

The world is in chaos. As a small business owner, you may have been trying to survive and get back to *normal*, but we're in a new world. Tried and true ways of running a business aren't going to work in the *new normal*. Too often, business owners fail to consider Diversity & Inclusion (D&I) as part of an overall strategic plan. From financials, to employee engagement, to product innovation – D&I is the one thread that ties all your business issues together.

D&I has not been effective in the past because we've tried to understand it through logic and facts. However, D&I is about people, and with people, we need to connect at the heart. In this chapter, you'll discover how *The Resilience Profitability Process*™ of Compassionate Diversity® can help you build a more effective, efficient, and inclusive business.

Chapter 4:
Flip the Paradigm:
Embrace the Human Approach to Boost Your Business
by Shalini Nag, Ph.D.

Nearly every Small Business Owner, entrepreneur, and business leader states that employees are their company's largest investment and most important asset. Yet, few are able to fully harness the potential of their people to achieve desired business outcomes.

This chapter reveals *The Success Delta*™ that sets exceptional companies apart, enabling them to tap into the discretionary effort of their people, and thrive in today's fast-changing business environment.

Wondering how you can transform your organization into an exceptional one? Look no further, because this chapter details the human approach of *Conversations for Business Success*™ and provides a comprehensive plan and specific action steps that you can take today.

Read this chapter so you, too, can learn how to have the right conversations, with the right people, at the right time, in the right manner. Transform your conversations and elevate your business today!

PERFORMANCE PILLAR 3: PRODUCTIVITY

Chapter 5:
Are Your Influencer Capabilities Being Overpowered
by Imposter Syndrome?
by Mike Raber

Did you know the majority of small business owners aren't aware their imposter syndrome holds them back from succeeding? I didn't either at first, now I know this firsthand. Stay with me, as I share *The 4 Secrets to Overcoming Imposter Syndrome*™.

Imposter syndrome can be a silent killer of true growth and success for small business owners and professionals. Do you find yourself having high aspirations; yet, feeling like somehow you don't fit in? What if I told you, the world needs you to share what you already have? It's true.

It wasn't until I had my back pushed up against the wall and started exploring all of who I was, what my own superpowers were, and my purpose for being here, that my truth was revealed. I then learned to embrace these four secrets as my business turned around. Now I'm sharing them with you:

- Own your expertise, don't fall prey to your insecurities!
- Whether or not you're an imposter, expert, or influencer, lies in your belief about yourself!
- What your mind can believe, through proper conditioning, you can achieve.
- Be coachable and trust your mentors or guides!

Chapter 6:
Integrate for Well-Managed, Intentional Growth
by Dennis Hill, Ph.D.

Knowledge is doubling every 12 hours due to globally networked technologies. Disruptions among paradigms and processes and their impact on your business change the *vaguely inevitable* into *immediately inescapable*, or you're out of business. Despite the variety of software programs available today, more than 80% of all small businesses employ pencil-and-paper for some routine information handling. Even if you're computerized with stand-alone programs for accounting or email marketing, isolated systems prevent the efficient transfer of common and valuable data. You can buy bridges to export and import data between these *islands of information*, but they breakdown when one or both program publishers make changes to their interfaces. In recent years, contact relationship software, e.g., Customer Relationship Management (CRM), has ranked as the top-selling software globally. Applying CRM-like techniques to more than sales, like workforce recruitment and supplier management, integrated processes will yield tremendous savings in labor, cost, and frustration.

Chapter 7:
Building Confidence Along with a Successful Business – From the Ground Up
by Melinda & Ryan Van Fleet

What are your dreams and goals? Are you confidently stepping into your potential on a regular basis? It's interesting to learn how most people are not living their potential. Confidence is a crucial component of fulfilling your dreams.

Confidence takes experience, trial, error, success, and patience, to name a few. It may seem scary, but everyone can become confident or build more confidence. Confidence can help you take action to achieve your goals, start or level up your business, build relationships, set boundaries, and manage your time.

This chapter is designed to inspire you with relatable stories and share tips of how others moved through various business challenges. They believe: if people would share more of their journey, others would realize they are not alone.

Is confidence stopping you from living your best life? Let this chapter put fear aside and help give you the encouragement to move forward. Don't let lack of confidence stop you!

PERFORMANCE PILLAR 4: PEACEFULNESS

Chapter 8:
Uncover Your Cells' Stories, Discover Your Quantum Nature™
You are the Best Asset of Your Business
by Jyun Shimizu, I-MD, Ph.D.

You are the best asset for your business. If you are not fully expressing the best version of yourself, how can you be successful in your business? The true *law of attraction* starts when you are authentic, positive, and optimistic. When you are surrounded by these resonances of vibration and frequency, your business and personal life's success will reflect and bring abundance. There are secret actions that will initiate a successful process.

The integration of *The 5 ISAMIZU Conscious Actions™* into your Conscious awareness of body, mind, and spirit, will unlock the infinite potentials that are hidden within yourself. Discover *Your Quantum Nature™* that is very specific and unique to you and create your highest performance that you desire.

Chapter 9:
How Valuing Your Values Adds Value to Your Business
by Rev. Maggie Mongan, CEO

Business textbooks don't address it. Most experts divert this subjective conversation. Only a few business advisors, who holistically approach business, will address this subtlety in the *Art of Business*; yet, the most successful business leaders and businesses diligently focus on identifying and activating their business' values into every aspect of their business.

Are you experiencing resistance, overwhelm, or frustration? Your beliefs, actions, or attitudes may be misaligned with your deep truths or values. Values are not goals, strategies, what you stand for, nor opinions. Think of values as what is most important to you. Values are your beliefs, attitudes, and behaviors. These beliefs are called values because you treasure them.

Discover how values impact your business operations and model, profitability, business relationships, branding and marketing messages, prioritization, culture, leadership and management, and your peace. Values keep you from drifting away from what matters most. Learn the foundational steps to *The Small Business Core Values Initial Inquiry*™. If identified and appropriately applied, values will add value to your life and business.

UNDERSTANDING OUR CHAPTER LAYOUT:

Introduction to the Chapters' Brilliant Practicing Expert™

As the Founder & Creator of this #1 Bestselling book series *Brilliant Breakthroughs for the Small Business Owner*, podcast, mobile app, and virtual summit, Maggie will introduce you to each chapter's author. She shares what makes the author unique via their skills and capabilities. Additionally, you will learn why the chapter's topic, through the lens of the author, matters to your business' performance.

Chapter Writing

Chapters are filled with tenured wisdom, proven tips, and experiences relevant to Small Business Owners (SBOs. We encourage you to learn and experiment to find your winning formula.

Chapter Glossary

All Brilliant Practicing Experts™ have terms they use in a particular fashion. Each chapter has a glossary to clarify what the author means as they impart their wisdom.

Author Biography Page

Each author wants you to become familiar with them. Included is a headshot, brief author description, and a free invitation to learn more about the topic they are addressing. This invitation is designed for you to learn more about the topic of their chapter.

Business Page

Each author's business is represented with an informative page for you to become familiar with the author's business. It contains a brief business description, and links for you to connect on their website and their social media accounts.

ADDITIONAL RESOURCES:

Book Purchases

This book is sold through Amazon.com and personally through each of the authors. For bulk orders, please contact Maggie Mongan at https://www.brilliantbreakthroughs.com/contact-us/.

To learn more about the authors, please go to: BrilliantBizBook at your mobile app store.

Here, you can meet all the authors online. Each Author's Page contains information about them and their business, as well as podcast interviews, videos, and social media links.

Engage with the Small Business Community on our app: BrilliantBizBook In addition to learning what is happening with our weekly podcast, annual summit, and happening authors, we have a community page for you to contribute what's happening with Small Business Owners. We're ready to hear your voice and learn how we can best support your success.

You have us on-demand in the palm of your hand once you access our mobile app!

Enjoy these fresh perspectives, meeting some *Brilliant Practicing Experts*™, and shining brightly!

PERFORMANCE
PILLAR 1

PROFITABILITY

Allow Me to Introduce Brilliant Practicing Expert™

Anne Mank, by Maggie Mongan

Once in a while, you bump into a person while networking and there's something special about them, which creates some mystique. Anne intrigued me – I knew there was something unique about her. We finally met after doing the calendar dance. I still wish the 90 minutes to eat and have our discovery conversation would've been twice as long.

Anne is one of those people who you know is a consummate professional with deep expertise running through her veins, but she doesn't flaunt it. Maybe it's her lifetime membership as a Girl Scout, or perhaps it was her practical approach to living, passion for the outdoors, or her commitment to her family.

Over time I've come to know Anne as an exceptional human who is here to better humankind. I'll share a secret with you: Anne's capabilities to be both analytical and creative surprised me. Usually, people with her background aren't as balanced in their approach to how they live and their profession. This is why Anne is the person you want to guide you while traversing your Financial Freedom Trail. Oh, did I mention she's pretty funny too? Make sure you take advantage of her offer at the bottom of her author's page and she'll take you on a unique journey.

The Financial Freedom Trail

by Anne Mank, CFP®, CPA

"Ok, deep breath, Annie. You've got this!" However, her breath became shallow. Her hands started to sweat as she stared at the trail in front of her to the extremely tall summit which had a fresh layer of snow covering the top. This was Annie's first official mountain hike. Her friends told her how great it would be to complete the Financial Freedom Trail, but at the moment, all she could think about was the warm and comfortable bed she left at 3:00 am.

"I must be crazy! Why did I think this would be a good idea?" Annie kept thinking. As she looked around, she noticed she was the first one there, and her guide was nowhere in sight. "Maybe I should go home. I don't need this. I don't need to prove anything to anyone, and actually, I quite enjoy my little walks through the city park. What am I doing?" Then she was filled with sadness as she thought about her friend Jill. Jill didn't deserve what happened to her, and Annie became terrified it would happen to her, as well. "That's it, I'm out of here!"

As she quickly turned around to leave, she came face to face with Victory. Now Victory wasn't your normal guide. She was confident, experienced, and you listened when she spoke. Annie was in awe of Victory and a little jealous. Annie has been working with Victory for the past four months in preparation for this hike. When Annie started hiking, she quickly realized she couldn't do this alone.

Sure, at first she thought she could. She bought the training app and set up a daily training routine for herself. Unfortunately, everything quickly became a disaster when she went for her first solo two-mile hike at the base of the mountain. Not only did she sprain her ankle, which was quite painful, but she didn't even think about the fact she might not have cell phone service in the woods. She had never been so scared or felt so helpless. She wasn't able to call anyone, her water supply ran very low, and it was dusk when she finally made her way out of the forest. A quick two-mile hike almost became a disaster.

How did you start your hike?

Starting your own business can be scary, overwhelming, and even painful at times. Often, you're leaving the comfort of a "good-paying" job to start on your journey. You might not even tell anyone you're starting this journey because you don't want them to see you fail. Actually, all your friends and families have only seen you succeed. What would it do to them if you didn't make it? According to Rebeccah Silence, Owner and Founder of Inspired Results, this is when, "You've got to get super clear about what it is you do and *why* you do it so that in the moments you think it'd be easier to throw in the towel, you can go back to your *why* and let that carry you through."[1]

Imagine, what if you had the right guide and tools to help you through this adventure? You might have a fighting chance! When looking for someone to work with, remember the coach is there to guide you and pull the answers out of you. You need to do the work. Rebeccah also stated, "You are responsible for the results you want to receive from coaching".[1] Additionally, Evelina Hovich, Integrative Holistic Life & Manifestation Coach, reminds us, "A good coach is the one who will help you discover the answers that are already within you."[2]

The Journey Continues...

"Annie, good morning! The weather is perfect for our hike and the views should be amazing! I think we will start on the southern path as we originally planned and then..." Victory's voice started to trail off. "Oh my goodness, Annie. What is the matter? You are as white as a ghost! Didn't you have breakfast?"

Annie responded so quickly and Victory only caught every third word. "I didn't sleep last night. I don't think my shoes fit me very well. Are you sure the southern path is best? What if I can't make it all the way? What do I do again if I have to use the bathroom? Will the views really be great? I am not sure it will be worth it."

"Whoa, Annie, take a breath. You have done such an awesome job training for this and You. Are. Ready." Victory reassured her. "Let's go over our checklist again. I think it will assure you."

The Financial Freedom Survival Kit™

- **Map:** Your visual plan for your destinations, the obstacles in your way, and how to track your progress. (Business Plan or Budget)
- **Compass:** When all else fails, your compass will guide you to your true north. Reminding you where you are going and how to get there. (Your WHY Statement)
- **Water:** This will keep you alive for days if there is an emergency. (Emergency Fund)
- **First Aid Kit:** If there is a fall or accident, this will patch you up and make sure you can get to your destination. This helps you prepare for those things making your journey more difficult without stopping you. (Strategies and Investment Diversification)
- **Food:** Your energy source. This will help you complete the hike while you stay healthy and enjoy the journey. (Revenue)
- **Guide:** That's me. I am here to teach you along the way so by the end of the journey, you are actually leading me to the top. (Wealth Coach)

Annie was starting to feel a little relieved at this point. She had spent a lot of time training and she constantly worked on the plan. She had all the tools, knew how to use them, and was starting to feel very confident. She was excited, determined, and joyful.

She skipped up the first couple of steps along the path. She felt like she was 10 years old again and was enjoying every second. Ah...the air was so crisp she was imagining her lungs were smiling back at her. Was that a deer on the hill? A bright red cardinal flew over her and rested on a branch as if to say, "You've got this."

"STOP!" Annie quickly snapped back to the moment. Annie looked down and noticed she was standing on a large rock which was on the edge of a small cliff. "Oh, my goodness! I wasn't paying attention! I got so caught up in the beauty and excitement of the woods I didn't even notice I was so close to the edge." Annie was a little shaken up but fine. "Thank you, Victory. I am so grateful you are with me. Even though I feel prepared and have all the right tools, I don't have the experience to know where the danger lies."

"This is what happened to my friend Jill. She was out for a hike by herself because she thought it was silly to pay someone to guide her on an easy walk. She thought anyone could do it. She was wrong and we almost lost her."

Victory then put her hand on Annie's shoulder to calm her down and noted, "I have fallen many times and have taken wrong turns, but each time I learned something new and became wiser. I'm here to help you learn from my mistakes so you can get to the summit faster and easier."

The Risk of Being the Business Owner

As a business owner, there is a lot of risk and uncertainty. You can't plan or prepare for every roadblock you face; however, do you have the support and network you need to help you get through those blocks? Most experiences aren't unique to us. There is probably someone who has been through it before.

Nancy Sparrow, Owner of Sparrow Solutions, shared, "Being in a business where you fully stand behind what you are delivering, how you are delivering it, and to whom you're delivering it, is the secret sauce."[3] Before you start your business, you need to fully understand *why* you are doing this. When times get scary or overwhelming, this will become your true north and guide you back to running a successful business.

Caution: You might try to build your business by yourself because you like the control, don't want to waste your money, or feel only you can do this.

Nancy Sparrow mentioned, "You don't have to know everything. In fact, I would say, it costs too much money for us to learn every skill. Take a look at the value equation and get support where it's going to bring exponential value."[3] Regardless of which phase you are in, you need to ask for help—and ask for it sooner rather than later.

Angela Johnson, Owner/Artist of BB Design, stated, "You really need to know what you're good at and what you're not good at. Then play to your strengths and find the right people, whether it's another business or you're hiring someone to fill the holes that you have."[4]

Hiking can be Dangerous

Victory looked up at the bright blue sky with big fluffy clouds floating past and announced they should stop for lunch. Annie protested and asked, "Can we keep going?" She was very eager to get to the top and was starting to feel a second wind. Besides, with the beautiful vista in front of them, why would Victory want to waste time by stopping to eat?

Victory asked Annie if she ever saw someone who was extremely dehydrated. She explained how the person will start to feel dizzy, their heart rate becomes rapid, they get confused and irritated, pass out, experience liver failure, and die. "It is a horrible way to die, so drink the water!" she urged.

How to Take Care of the Business

As a small business owner, you have plenty of responsibilities. Your primary responsibility is to yourself; the secondary is to those who sign up to work with you. You must make sure you have enough energy and resources to successfully make the journey.

How much of an emergency fund have you created for yourself and separately for your business? Are you putting away cash to pay taxes quarterly? When was the last time you consistently paid yourself a salary?

You need to follow the money much like water going over a waterfall—it's *The Cashflowing Model*™. Imagine you are looking at three waterfalls flowing from a large lake at the top of the mountain.

The first waterfall covers all your tax responsibilities (income, payroll, sales). **Remember:** If there is a transaction between two parties, it will have a tax attached to it and money will flow down this waterfall.

The second waterfall would be for the business operations. You will use these funds for technology, marketing, or inventory. Whatever you need to make the business run should come from this waterfall. **Remember:** to include future expansion like opening a second location or adding additional offerings. Katrina Potter, Owner of Life Fuel, wisely states, "One of the biggest mistakes Small Business Owners make about money is they focus on the right here and right now versus looking at it from a long-term play."[5]

The third waterfall would be for you. One of the biggest mistakes business owners make is not paying themselves. If the business can't survive without paying you, then you should create a better solution. You should always pay yourself a salary AND save for a rainy day.

Remember your physical and mental health, as well. When was the last time you took a vacation day? Are you burning out your employees? To have a successful business for the long term, you must have processes in place and services which don't involve you. A successful five-year goal for the business would be to have it run without you.

Annie is Taking Over

Victory now has Annie take the lead. Annie is looking around and noticing the beauty, but also considering what might go wrong. She is starting to anticipate difficulties in their path and successfully navigating them. Annie hasn't even noticed Victory is slowly giving her more space because, at this point, Annie is on her own. Victory is there to support her and watch over her, but it is now up to Annie to complete the rest of the journey.

Completely out of breath, Annie is climbing the steepest part of the path. Just a couple more steps and there it is...it's beauty beyond words. Annie stops, stares, and takes it all in. Tears start streaming down her cheek because she made it. It is even better than she could have ever imagined. Definitely worth the training, effort, and sacrifice. She takes in the view and is absolutely filled with gratitude.

Victory slowly walks up by Annie and whispers, "Beyond words, isn't it?" Annie nods her head. Then Victory points to a higher summit in the distance declaring, "That one is next." Annie agrees, "Let's do it!"

What is Success for You?

Those first steps in starting a business may be the hardest. Typically, it's business owners who stop themselves. Why is this? It's because of the stories and the *survival personality* we have created for ourselves when it comes to money and success.

Recall who first taught you about money? What were some of the emotions you remember about those stories? If money was a person, would it be your friend or enemy? To what level of success have you given yourself permission to attain money?

I challenge you to think positive thoughts about money. If you have a cell phone bill to pay, be thankful for all the people you were able to connect with. When you look at your bank statement, instead of thinking, "It is never enough," think about how much you have compared to most people in the world. Evelina Hovich says it well: "There is an unlimited amount of money, opportunities, and clients. Whether we manifest it into our reality or not, will depend on our thoughts, beliefs, and inspired actions."[2]

Annie, like many business owners, learned many valuable life skills during the climb; yet, it was the guide, tools, and plan which made the climb successful. Have you set yourself up for success? Will you be able to make it to your summit of The Financial Freedom Trail?

The Financial Freedom Trail
Glossary:

Budget: A forward-looking estimate of the sales and expenses of the business which is then compared to the actual activity each month.

Business Plan: Is a plan detailing the goals of the business, and the anticipated steps and processes needed to achieve those goals.

Emergency Fund: Money set aside to cover financial surprises.

Investment Diversification: Investment plan which incorporates various risk levels and investment products to meet your individual needs.

Revenue: Income produced from the sale of products or services and is also referred to as gross sales.

Strategy: Is a framework for making decisions to achieve a long-term goal.

Survival Personality: The personality you created to survive your childhood or trauma in your life.

Wealth Coach: Individual who guides you in finding clarity around your financial goals and developing financial strategies that align with your core values.

Your Why Statement: It is your purpose and what inspires you to take action.

Meet Brilliant Practicing Expert™ Anne Mank:

Certified Financial Planner™
CPA | Integrative Holistic Coach | Wealth Coach

Anne Mank, CFP®, CPA, is based in Wisconsin. Anne's 20+ years of industry experience has taken her around the world, helping companies with her accounting, financial, and compliance expertise. Anne knows there is nothing more powerful than a woman who understands the language of money, and she is committed to disrupting the money conversation to help them live a better than ordinary life.

ANNE'S SPECIAL INVITATION FOR YOU:

Start your journey on The Financial Freedom Trail by requesting your free trail guide at **https://www.betterthanordinary.com/BBguide.**

Business: Better Than Ordinary, LLC

As a financial advisor Anne has been blessed to be able to help hundreds of individuals work towards their financial goals. Through this work, she noticed the lack of education around money and finances, especially for women. This is how Better Than Ordinary, LLC was born.

Better Than Ordinary is a place where people, and especially women, can come to learn about money, wealth, and finance in a safe and caring environment. We help educate and coach individuals towards their financial goals without the shame, judgment, or embarrassment they might feel somewhere else. The ultimate goal is to empower women to understand the language of money so they can live a Better Than Ordinary life.

Website: https://www.betterthanordinary.com

Connect with Anne on these social accounts:
LinkedIn: https://www.linkedin.com/in/annemank/
Instagram: https://www.instagram.com/better_than_ordinary/

**Download Mobile App: BrilliantBizBook from your App Store.
It contains everything related to this Book Series and its Authors.**

Allow Me to Introduce Brilliant Practicing Expert™

Mark Boeder, by Maggie Mongan

If you know Mark Boeder, the next sentence will make you smile. Mark and I initially met networking over 10 years ago and last year we bumped into each other again at another event. Just as Mark teaches, he practices what he preaches.

Since I was an executive recruiter and talent acquisition partner for almost a decade, I understand how unique the industry is and who truly has the right approach to appropriately support companies. Great recruiters are masterful – they've taken years to perfect their expertise and marketplace. They are the secret keepers of what's happening in industry. Only few, like Mark, are the invisible hand behind a business's success.

For the past four years I've been searching for a tenured recruiter with the right background to share their wisdom with Small Business Owners. Why? There is no room for a mis-hiring error in small business. If you don't get this right, your profitability may not recover.

Listen to Mark – especially how to create your business's ongoing search team and strategies. Additionally, make sure to take advantage of his next steps at the bottom of his author's page. You'll be glad you have this forward-thinking approach and his tenure to lean on.

Uplevel Your Business by Replacing Your Irreplaceable Employees: Move to Indispensable Key Talent for Ultimate Success

by Mark Boeder

Your approach today determines your business's future success. Irreplaceable employees or Indispensable Key Talent—Your choice is vitally important.

Do you want to grow your business exponentially? Whether your organization is enterprise-scale, midsize, or smaller, the same holds true - you need to begin by replacing those people you have thought of as "irreplaceable" with those who are *Indispensable Key Talent*.

Today, unprecedented changes are transforming virtually every aspect of how people work and how hiring occurs. Organizations cannot only pay lip service to being innovative when it comes to executive search, but they must also adapt to the changes in the marketplace and be proactive.

Having top people in the right roles is critical to the survival of your business. Even more critical is having the appropriate individuals in your organization understand the effort it will take to find the *right high-impact business professionals* to carry your organization into the future. Finding these people is the challenge. In the war for talent, you need to focus on finding high-impact hires to create an environment of success.

Understanding there is a big difference between the merely irreplaceable and those business professionals deemed indispensable is integral to building an executive search machine (or engaging with one) which will enable you to find the *Indispensable Key Talent* to exponentially grow your company.

The key here is to mind the gap between a person considered to be *"irreplaceable"* versus the kind of person who is truly indispensable is not one of *degree*, but rather a difference in *kind*. *Indispensable Key Talent* is a completely different breed of talent. *Indispensable Key Talent* will help you grow exponentially. Those considered "irreplaceable" will fool you into a sense of believing everything is being handled—even though there are embers smoldering in the back room!

The Impact of Indispensable Key Talent

No matter their job function, *Indispensable Key Talent* is able to deliver tremendous impact. Being indispensable is a characteristic rather than a skill.

Being indispensable is a mindset. It demonstrates the way one sees and reacts to problems and allows a business professional to focus their skills and expertise on solving the problem(s) rather than focusing on details and functions in a role.

In a blog post, Amber Nusland differentiated the *indispensable* versus the mere *irreplaceable*. "Indispensable people are the types that you can hand any project, put in nearly any role, issue a challenge to, and they simply make things happen by understanding what needs to get done and adapting their skills accordingly." [1]

Nusland continues, "Being irreplaceable is the opposite. It's about being locked into a role because the person is harboring finite knowledge, skills, or information they can't or aren't willing to share with anyone else. Sometimes that is borne from insecurity. Other times it's a false sense that if you protect your sandbox, so that only you know its secrets, you have job security for life."

But as we all know, the irreplaceable *always* get replaced due to technology or automation, etc., because their skills become commonplace. The skills become a commodity because skills are not doing anything game changing, but rather just keeping the lights on. Conversely, people, and more specifically those who are *Indispensable Key Talent*, are the game changers.

The way to build a resilient and powerful business is by finding and wooing some of those indispensable people, at least indispensable for a foreseeable future, to join your organization so you can leverage their *best stuff*. Search, discovery, and onboarding of these people, the *franchise players*, around whom you build the rest of your organization, enables you to build a team who can be inspired to navigate uncharted waters without you.

Find and Hire Skilled and Adaptable People Who are Smarter Than You

Hire people smarter than yourself. Share with them what YOU know and then remove the obstacles for them so they can bring their best selves to do compelling, rare, crucial, and essential work.

I advocate for a key talent-seeking approach to be used in a universal fashion rather than as a functional-area-specific checklist of skills for a qualified candidate for a particular job or title. Look for smart people, thinkers who see other ways of solving problems (big or small) in all aspects of their work, home, and play. These are the people who are adaptable and at their best when confronted with a dumpster fire of a business problem. They don't operate from a manual. Their skills are unique and evolve over time. Very few businesses can sustain growth or thrive without some of these business professionals.

To grow a company exponentially, it is imperative to find *Indispensable Key Talent* who are amazingly good at what they do.

No matter if your company is a small business or large enterprise, the competitive edge demanded by the marketplace for your company to thrive, and even grow exponentially, are people who are more human, more connected with others, and more emotionally intelligent in their dealings.

Companies should be seeking:

- A professional with fervor and intensity, while having a capacity for seeing abstract ideas as real things.
- A person who is able to arbitrate, mediate, and negotiate multiple prerogatives, and who makes decisions without fear, uncertainty, or doubt.
- Someone resilient and adaptable in the face of transformational forces, both internal and external.
- A person who gets *sh$t* done.

NOTE: This talent is **not** a person whom the Human Resources Department will be able to find by "posting and praying," as most companies still do today. To move to the next level and grow, a company in search of key talent needs to understand the company's and team's needs, goals, and expectations in order to undertake the discovery and delivery of exceptional candidates who possess very similar needs, goals, and expectations.

According to Cindy Bacskai, VP of Talent Management for Essentia Health, "A do-it-yourself approach can derail you. Get experts to help find the right people. One bad hire can really have a huge effect on a small business."[2]

Finding key talent needs to be a full-time, long-term, and sustained effort. It is not about a *just-in-time* recruitment approach. It is not about job descriptions, nor titles. It is about building long-term relationships with indispensable people. You may find them in your local professional community, a nationwide vertical-focused community, or a virtual professional community. Regardless of where they are, they make up the pool of people with the *right stuff,* and their own connections, to help you find diamonds in the rough.

Where do you find Indispensable Key Talent?

To find these folks, one needs to find the right *rooms* they inhabit. These *rooms* could be an actual room, a virtual room, or a business-focused affinity group, where members share a common interest or passion. *Hunting* for the right rooms is the first external step of the process and entails a great amount of networking and communicating with people to find out where indispensable people congregate or can be found.

It is highly unlikely one will happen to just bump into the candidate of your dreams in one of these rooms; however, within the group, it *is* highly likely there are a number of people who are connected to, and influential with, the kind of people with whom you want to communicate. Sometimes the focus on this activity is difficult for the hiring manager to do well.

"Outsource the skills and knowhow you need. A search firm can really help," says Klint Kendrick, Director of Strategic Workforce Initiatives for SC Johnson. "Establishing relationships with search firms who focus on your areas of need is best. They have the expertise and contacts. The hiring manager should focus on what they do well and outsource the effort to an expert."[3]

INSIGHT: If your endeavor is to increase the quality and growth of your business, you must develop the capability, or outsource the effort, to maintain this ongoing search activity. Even if you choose not to use an external expert for this activity, your *Indispensable Key Talent Search Team*™ must plan and execute the search for these kinds of people on a nonstop basis. The sole focus is to find and develop relationships, stay in contact, and stay relevant with the *Indispensable Key Talent* required to consistently grow your business. Seeking, surfacing, and delivering highly-skilled people, when and how you need them most, is *strategic* and must be the sole focus of your *Indispensable Key Talent Search Team*™.

NOTE: For your *Indispensable Key Talent Search Team*™ to have legitimacy for the key talent whom they are seeking and engaging, the team members must qualify as *Indispensable Key Talent themselves*.

TIP: To ensure success, there must be agreement regarding your business's goals, mission, and initiatives. This is the first internal step in finding the appropriate people. Be sure there is a universal understanding among your team regarding the organizational needs and budget. Determining who is the authority to make decisions relative to your business, your culture, and your business needs is paramount.

Lou Adler, CEO, and Founder of the Adler Group and Performance-based Hiring Learning Systems, shared, "Define the work as a series of job objectives. Define performance objectives. Don't start looking until you define the work."[4]

CAUTION: A just-in-time recruiting and hiring process will not help you find the best candidates—it sets you up to settle for only acceptable candidates who happen to be available at the time of your need. A company which is ready to be competitive in finding the *difference makers*, the *game chang*ers, the *franchise players*, and the *Indispensable Key Talent* to grow will only evolve if you are committed to building and nurturing long-term relationships with potential candidates and influencers in your marketplace.

Your company must hire and/or designate one person or a small team (*The Indispensable Key Talent Search Team™*) or outsource the effort to a business partner who will spearhead this relationship-building and sourcing of people to ensure effectiveness. This person or team, alongside your hiring managers, needs to develop a *strategy* for each search. This person or team develops a long-range strategy to continue to find and develop relationships with *Indispensable Key Talent* as a part of their daily accountabilities.

Sharif Mansur, an Organizational Development and Professional Training expert, believes that a company needs to utilize "a separate Talent Acquisition person or team who do *not* also have responsibilities of an HR Generalist; this should be someone whose sole job is Talent Acquisition, whether that person is internal or if the process is outsourced."[5]

Can you afford not to hire top talent?

The cost of **not** hiring top talent is far greater than the cost of Indispensable Key Talent. Hiring *Indispensable Key Talent* needs to be seen as a strategic undertaking for your company. This is not a task for a traditional Human Resources Department. Your *Indispensable Key Talent Search Team™* must be dedicated to finding people who, above all else, differentiate themselves in many ways from other candidates. Focus on the way candidates think, view the world, and problem solve.

TIP: A candidate's first impression of your business often comes from HR or the visible parts of your search apparatus. If they feel like the hiring process is simply transactional and they are a commodity, they will not be interested in your opportunity nor business. They want to feel someone genuinely cares about them, seek an opportunity to create, and determine whether or not your company might meet *their* expectations.

The Accountabilities for *The Indispensable Key Talent Search Team*™:

- Establish and maintain a network of industry contacts through participation in professional/trade associations and other professional networking organizations for leads and introductions to *Indispensable Key Talent*.
- Consistently find and develop relationships with high impact professionals.
- Introduce themselves and your business to Key Talent as part of the networking and connecting process.
- Assess potential candidates to ensure qualification match, cultural fit, and overall compatibility with business requirements.
- Build a strategic and unified communication plan for each potential candidate.
- Build a process for bringing candidates into a formal interview process when the timing is right.

Essentials for Successful Talent Search & Recruitment Operations™

- Analyze hiring needs.
- Partner with the hiring manager to define strategic objectives and hiring needs.
- Determine the best-recruiting methods.

- Create and deploy client-specific and/or role-specific recruiting strategies and tactics.
- Build and maintain subject matter expertise on target industries, clients, and roles.
- Conduct behavioral-based interviews and competency-based evaluations.
- Provide guidance and facilitate the negotiation process.
- Complete candidate hiring and on-boarding processes in accordance with organizational requirements.

REMEMBER: None of this occurs until *after* you, and those whom you task with the search for *Indispensable Key Talent*, have begun to establish a meaningful relationship with high-impact top talent. It is imperative for you and your organization to build and maintain a comprehensive network and pipeline of Key Talent to address your organization's ongoing needs. This process might require a couple of years before it is fully developed.

It's Your Choice: Plan to Grow or Slowly Die

If your company is not growing, it is slowly going out of business.

Extraordinary shifts are revolutionizing how business is successfully being conducted today. Every facet of performance is being scrutinized. The one constant? Your people as your competitive advantage. As difficult as it may be to develop a process and attract *Indispensable Key Talent*, the effects of not doing it will create greater difficulties. By developing a stellar process to attract your *Indispensable Key Talent Search Team™,* you will support your business's future success.

Regardless of your business's size, you have advantages and disadvantages. Larger businesses have more employees to participate in these activities; yet, their bureaucracy hampers timeliness. Small businesses have fewer resources; however, they are more resilient to take action when *Indispensable Key Talent* presents itself.

Make no mistake—there *is* a war for talent! Business owners and leaders must create an environment of success by constantly searching for *Indispensable Key Talent* for your business's success, growth, and profitability. Now, you have a choice: you can develop and manage this pipeline or have it built and maintained by a professional with executive-search experience. This is no longer optional—you benefit by choosing a path today. Your business's growth and profitability depend on your securing *Indispensable Key Talent*—use this as a best practice to support your business's future.

Uplevel Your Business by Replacing Your Irreplaceable Employees Move to Indispensable Key Talent for Ultimate Success

Glossary:

Behavioral-based interviews: Interviewing technique which employers use to evaluate candidate's past behavior in different situations in order to predict their future performance.

Candidate: Contender for a job.

Competency-based evaluations: An assessment that provides a way of measuring and building the skills and knowledge people need to perform their job.

Competitive edge: A factor that gives a company an advantage over rivals and competitors.

Culture: Shared attitudes and behavior characteristics of a particular business.

Emotionally intelligent: *Emotional intelligence,* aka *emotional quotient* or EQ, is the ability to understand, use, and manage one's own *emotions* in positive ways to relieve stress, communicate effectively, empathize with others, overcome challenges and defuse conflict.

Executive Search: Executive search, aka is a specialized recruitment service that organizations pay to seek out and recruit highly qualified candidates for senior-level and executive jobs.

Executive search machine: Specialized search function designed to find highly qualified candidates for senior-level and executive jobs.

Exponential growth: Rapid and aggressive advancement.

Franchise player/game-changer: A highly skilled person around whom you build a high-performance team.

High impact business professionals: Individuals with the biggest dreams, the greatest potential to create things that matter and grow, while inspiring others.

Hiring Manager: Person with a need, budget, and authority to make a hiring decision.

Hiring onboarding process: The processes to ensure new hires get started favorably.

Hiring process: Process of finding, selecting, and hiring new employees to a company

Hunting: The act of searching, identifying, and approaching a suitable person to fill a business position.

Interview process: The interview process typically includes creating a job description, publicizing the job, scheduling and conducting interviews, following up with candidates, and making a hire.

Indispensable Key Talent: Adaptable, high impact professionals who deliver tremendous impact no matter their job function.

Indispensable Key Talent Search Team™: A search team specifically designed for hunting for high impact business professionals the company may want to hire one day.

Irreplaceable employees: Employees who harbor finite knowledge, skills, or information they can't or aren't willing to share with anyone else. In actuality, they are *very* replaceable.

Just-in-time recruitment: A hiring methodology that provides hiring managers with candidates to match their specifications as needed; reactive rather than proactive.

Needs/goals/expectations: The business reasons behind why a position in a company exists and are used to measure the promise and performance of a new hire.

Negotiation process: Method by which compromise or agreement is reached while avoiding argument and dispute, often with regard to expectations of responsibilities or benefits of a job.

Posting and praying: A common and passive recruitment approach many recruiters and hiring managers in which they *post* a position to a job board then *pray* the best candidate will apply.

Recruitment: Action of finding new people to join an organization.

Right rooms: Places, either real or virtual, where the kind of influential and connected people can be found to help you connect with top-level talent.

Right stuff: Personal attributes, or character traits, considered necessary to succeed or do something well.

Successful Talent Search and Recruitment Operations Essentials™: The basics of talent search and recruitment that must be at a high level of excellence and capability so that you can unleash the Indispensable Key Talent Search Team™ to do their work; the structure of high-quality Talent Search and Recruitment Operations must exist before you uplevel.

Top talent: Business professionals with high aptitude or skill.

War for talent: Refers to an increasingly competitive landscape for search, discovery, communication, assessment, hiring, and retaining of super *talented* high impact employees.

Meet Brilliant Practicing Expert™ Mark Boeder:

Executive Search Consultant | Job Search | Interview Authority & Guide Connector of Businesses & Professionals

Mark Boeder, the founder and Key Talent GPS of WarHorse Executive Search, has built a team that possesses a very positive, contagious attitude along with a professional image, and demeanor allowing them to connect with the Executive Level and *Indispensable Key Talent* with whom YOU might wish to communicate. He seeks, surfaces, and delivers High Impact Key Talent crucial to a company's growth. As the Key Talent GPS, Mark is the bridge between *Indispensable Key Talent* and organizations who are obsessed with growth. Raised in a small town in Wisconsin, he possesses an extremely strong Midwestern Work Ethic, integrity, and personal energy. Mark is a business leader and connector who has found thousands of great candidates who have helped companies grow during his 25 years in the industry.

MARK'S SPECIAL INVITATION FOR YOU:

Mark invites you to learn more about how WarHorse Executive Search can help find the *Indispensable Key Talent* your company needs to grow, or he can help you develop your own capabilities for doing so. **Connect with Mark at https://warhorseexecutivesearch.com**

Business: WarHorse Executive Search

Having top people in the right roles is critical to the survival and success of your organization. At WarHorse Executive Search, we call this *Indispensable Key Talent*. We match talent, who is highly motivated to make an immediate and transformational impact, to companies that are looking for exponential growth.

You're looking for a professional with fervor and intensity, a capacity for seeing abstract ideas as real things and plainly - someone who gets it done. We call this *Indispensable Key Talent* and it is what you need to take your company to the next level.

WarHorse Executive Search partners with companies to define strategic objectives and needs and match them to a candidate with the right skills. Beyond that, we connect you to the talent that wants to make a difference.

**Websites: https://www.warhorseexecutivesearch.com
https://www.warhorsetalent.com**

Connect with Mark on these social accounts:

Twitter: https://twitter.com/WarHorseTalent/
https://twitter.com/markboeder/
Instagram: https://www.instagram.com/warhorse_talent/
LinkedIn: https://www.linkedin.com/in/markboeder/

**Download Mobile App: BrilliantBizBook from your App Store.
It contains everything related to this Book Series and its Authors.**

PERFORMANCE
PILLAR 2

PEOPLE

Allow Me to Introduce Brilliant Practicing Expert™
Susan McCuistion, by Maggie Mongan

We welcome one of our returning authors, Susan McCuistion, who wrote in Volume 1 about the *Five Ways to Bring Compassion to Your Organization*. In that chapter, she built a researched case revealing how we haven't evolved as much as we perceive we have regarding the *people thing*.

For over 25 years, Susan's conversations focus on how our conscious and unconscious beliefs and behaviors about people impact all our relationships. She invites us to move beyond the intellectual approach, which isn't working. Instead, she stands in her conviction for a new approach – through the heart, focusing on compassion. Humanity will appreciate our efforts with this new approach.

As a Small Business Owner, your people, productivity, profit, and peacefulness are impacted by the lenses of your *people perception*. With each hire, you add more lenses of perception to your business. Learning how to appropriately process all the diverse richness you have presented within your team will minimize the hidden costs impacting your profit. Remember to engage with Susan to learn more about this new approach by click on her invitation at the bottom of her author's page.

The Hidden Cost of Doing Business

by Susan McCuistion

The world is in chaos. As a global family, the COVID-19 pandemic is changing the way we work, go to school, and interact with each other. Freedoms we took for granted are being limited; the safety of something as simple as going out to a restaurant is being questioned, and small businesses have been left devastated.

Here in the United States, rising anger from hundreds of years of systemic injustices have resulted in both peaceful protests and riots which have spread globally. Social media has allowed access to killings and riots in real-time, traumatizing all who watch. Deborah Levine, Editor-in-Chief, American Diversity Report, affirms, "[Diversity, Equity, and Inclusion (DEI)] has been changed dramatically given COVID, [Black Lives Matter], and our extraordinarily divided society. The resulting anxiety and pessimism make the work of DEI professionals both more necessary and more difficult."[1]

While I have been doing Diversity & Inclusion (D&I) work for nearly 25 years, I am a mathematician by education. Chaos theory states, despite what we are observing, *there is an underlying order*. Think about a caterpillar as it creates its chrysalis. It melts down into a soupy liquid–complete chaos–to reorder and emerge as a beautiful butterfly.

As a small business owner, you're probably not so confident *order* is underlying all of the changes you are going through. You may have been trying to survive and get back to *normal*, but we're in a new world. Tried and true ways of running a business aren't going to work in the *new normal*. To build our business for the future, we must tear down what's inefficient and ineffective in order to create a new foundation to be more effective and increase the bottom line.

What's *really* causing your business issues?

Business issues are not necessarily unique. Too often, we look at these issues in a silo. As John Barth, Deputy CFO, Transportation Security Administration, states, these issues come down to one thing:

> Regardless of where you work, or what you do, the common denominator is people. Those people can be employees or customers. It would make sense to most of us that employees and customers who feel valued and appreciated will keep coming back and contributing to the success of the enterprise, probably providing free, positive advertising along the way. Demonstrating a commitment to D&I in every aspect of your business is the easiest and most productive way to achieve the positive results that every organization and leader strives for.[2]

From financials, to employee engagement, to product innovation– diversity and inclusion ties it all together. Amri Johnson, Executive Advisor, A. Johnson Partners asserts:

> Weaving D&I into every aspect of a business can sound like a platitude when there has historically been little progress in D&I efforts. If a business wants inclusion to happen, it will think about it systemically like it does any priority. It takes an organization that understands the fundamentals of inclusion and then weaves the behavioral skills and structural design needed into business systems to bolster business capacity.[3]

Too often, business owners fail to consider D&I as part of an overall strategic plan. We're really good at assuming everybody else is just like us, only to learn while working on a difficult project, in the heat of a conflict, or while having a simple discussion, they aren't.

Until we're able to admit we're just not as good at connecting with people as we *think* we are, we can't even begin to understand how D&I is at the root of our business issues.

The science of bias and disconnection

I am an eternal optimist. I believe 99% of us wake up in the morning with good intentions to go to work, make a decent living, take care of our families, connect with our friends, and help our communities. I don't believe we wake up intentionally trying to hurt others, yet we inevitably do. Why?

We don't understand our biases and how our perspectives exclude others.

One of the concepts people are most resistant to in the field of D&I is bias. "You're biased!" is typically thrown out as an insult. We all want to believe we aren't biased. However, *we are all biased*. It's how our brains work. Research shows our brains process about 11 million pieces of information at any given time, yet it can only handle about 50.[4] Our brain is set up to gather new information in unfamiliar situations and compare it to data it has gathered in the past. Bias is simply a preference for a particular way of doing, or thinking about, things.

It's not the bias that matters. Bias just makes us human. It's what we *do* with our biases that can positively or negatively impact our businesses and lives. Shrivallabh K points out:

> The world today is poised at an interesting juncture...Society is greatly reactive today and that makes it even easier to be influenced by opinions and stories on Social Media...How

does one react to someone who discloses their Covid-19 positive status (or any illness for that matter), or how does one react to a person from a community being targeted by the cops would largely depend on how they would respond to what they see and hear from others, from Social Media.[5]

I don't believe we can solve these issues unless we understand what's happening from a holistic point of view. We are all part of the system, and we are all connected.

In communities where high levels of bias exist, people are less likely to trust and bond with each other, leading to a lack of social connectedness. This lack of connection is more detrimental to our health than obesity, smoking, and high blood pressure.[6] Physical acts of bias and discrimination take a mental and emotional toll on everyone involved – victims, perpetrators, and observers. Note:

- Researchers have found exclusion is processed by the brain as physical pain.[7] When we are rejected socially, our brains release the same opioids into our systems that are released when we experience physical pain. These natural pain killers help ease the mental and emotional pain we feel from such dismissals.

- When racism, sexism, and homophobia are brought to the attention of those engaging in such behavior, they experience a strong mix of negative emotions, such as fear and guilt, blocking their ability to develop further awareness and ultimately leading to avoidance and defensiveness.[8]

- Simply watching an event triggers a special class of neurons in our brain to engage. Mirror neurons are brain cells that fire not only when we do something, but also when we observe someone else doing something.[9] For example, when you see someone else stubbing their toe, the mirror neurons remind you of the pain you felt when you stubbed your toe, and you flinch. It's these same mirror neurons that fire when we witness traumatic events–like someone being beaten. The neurons fire and our brain reacts as if we're being beaten. Cortisol, adrenaline, and other harmful hormones and chemicals are released into our system.[10] The result is not only empathy for the other person, but also added stress on our own bodies.

What's compassion got to do with diversity?

While there have been a few adjustments here and there, we tend to teach D&I the same way we did years ago–through logic and facts. There have been endless articles written about why diversity training doesn't work. After over 20 years in this field, I know why:

- We force people through classes, piling on guilt for some while leaving others feeling justified.
- We don't teach a subject which is all *about people* in a way that actually *connects with* people. We teach to the head, not to the heart.
- We fail to make connections for people about the personal benefits of things like self-awareness and understanding others.

We're not good at talking about diversity because we've not been taught to do so. We grow up being told it's "not polite" to ask people certain questions or to talk about certain topics. As a result, we assume everyone has similar interpretations for basic values in life–like respect, integrity, or excellence. Except, we don't. We may *value* the same things, but *how we express those values* may be quite different.

It's common to believe, "I treat other people like I want to be treated," is the best course of action, but what if other people don't *want* to be treated the way you want to be treated? Wouldn't it be more respectful to treat others the way *they* wanted to be treated?

What's this mean for business?

When we assume someone is, "just like me," we assume they have the same wants, needs, and motivations. We decide who is (and isn't) qualified for a job based on whether or not they act like we do. We coach them by telling them what worked for us. We measure their performance by our own preferences for how things get done. We assume the products and services successful in one market should work in a new market. In the end, we miss out on good employees, squash innovation, and lose sales.

This is where Compassionate Diversity® comes in. Compassionate Diversity® is a comprehensive approach to seeing different perspectives, understanding others, and building bridges in understanding which incorporates both the head and the heart. We develop compassion and affect change through understanding what others truly need *from their perspective–not what we think they need.*

Fundamental to Compassionate Diversity® is *The Resilience Profitability Process*™ (RPP):

- At the **Comprehension** level, we work to understand the reactions and expectations of ourselves and others, and the purpose and outcomes of the situation.
- At the **Connection** level, we work to create shared meaning and alignment of purpose.
- In **Collaboration**, we develop more innovative and sustainable solutions in our businesses and our communities by creating more compassionate environments.

Putting the RPP into Action

The RPP moves compassion into action. Whenever we're in a new situation or place of conflict, we can use this process to effectively move forward.

First, the ground rules:

1. **All perspectives are valid even if you don't agree with them.** We all come to our viewpoints through complex processes informed by our learning and experiences in life. No path, therefore no perspective, is less valid than any other.

2. **Your focus is to understand, inform, and resolve.** You are not trying to convince anyone of anything, because right/ wrong arguments lead to polarization.

3. **It's okay not to know.** We live in a world where saying, "I don't know," or, "Let me get back to you," means we're stupid, or we don't know what we're doing. Inclusion work requires vulnerability. Vulnerability allows us the space necessary to say, "I don't know." This can be difficult to do, especially for business leaders, but *admitting our vulnerability helps to build trust.*[11]

Comprehension

The first step in *Comprehension* is emotional awareness. Our emotions are our internal guidance system. They tell us whether we are in or out of alignment with our beliefs, values, and expectations (BVE). If we're feeling good in a particular situation, then it means we are in alignment with our BVE. If we're not feeling so good, then we're out of alignment. It's that simple.

Next, take inventory of your BVE. What are your beliefs about the situation? What are your expectations? What might others involved be thinking and feeling?

Now, we need to understand the deeper purpose and desired outcomes of the situation. For instance, if we're interviewing a candidate, then the purpose isn't to ask questions and gather answers. Our purpose is to find the best person for the job. How might our biases get in the way of accomplishing this purpose?

Connection

We want to use the information we gathered in *Comprehension* to create shared meaning and alignment to purpose. It's important we connect before there's a bigger gap in understanding and we miss out on the next sale, lose another employee, or allow conflict to get out of hand. CAUTION: *We are not trying to solve anything at this stage.* Resist the temptation to jump in with any conclusions. We may even need to occasionally circle back to *Comprehension* as we go through this *Connection* step.

First, decide what is out of alignment. Are your BVE out of alignment with the purpose of the situation? Are your BVE out of alignment with others? We often try to change people to conform to our perspective when it's the process, or maybe even us, that needs to change. If it's you who needs straightening out, then get into alignment with the purpose of the situation and move on to *Collaboration*.

If alignment is necessary with others, then it is time to begin conversations. Remember the ground rules of this process, and first identify the things you have in common. You may find the gap is not as wide as you perceived. Once you have found common ground, then begin to talk about the differences.

Don't default into defending your position. Instead, ask questions like:

- "Can you tell me more?"
- "What else would you like me to know about this?"
- "What more do you want to know from me?"

CRITICAL: *Listen to understand and resist every urge you have to refute what you're hearing.* Doing so only ends up polarizing the discussion, deteriorating trust, and increasing frustration. When you're feeling frustrated and want to jump in, focus on your heart, and slow down your breathing. Shifting the focus to our hearts gets us out of our heads and helps us to think more clearly by bringing our heart rhythm into a more coherent state.

Finally, don't expect the other person to be the only one to change. Be open to modifying your own expectations along the way.

Collaboration

When we understand the situation and we feel we have all the information we need to make an appropriate decision, then we can move on to *Collaboration*. Here, we take appropriate action to drive desired outcomes. There are only two outcomes: 1) change; or, 2) no change. "Change" means we need to create a new process or system. "No change" means we maintain the status quo, but with a new understanding. This may mean having to accept some things we may not agree with or letting go of other long-held beliefs.

Creating the new normal

The old way of doing D&I isn't working. This is our chrysalis moment—our opportunity to emerge anew. This is not a time to carry forward worn out and ineffective practices around D&I or get back to an ineffective *normal*. It's our opportunity to create systems and practices which are truly inclusive in order to build more engaged and productive workplaces.

Through compassion, we can affect the changes we need to make in our businesses and our world.

The Hidden Cost of Doing Business
Glossary:

Barriers: Any block to equal treatment for a group of people. Some barriers may be historic – e.g. handed down through history, such as practices around segregation – and others may be systemic – e.g. built within the system, such as recruiting or interview practices that are intentionally or unintentionally built to exclude certain groups of people.

Bias: Learned patterns of behavior and/or thinking that create our preferences. We may be aware (conscious) or unaware (unconscious of our biases. Our biases are informed by our personal learning and experience, social cues, and the media.

Black Lives Matter (BLM: A political and social movement focused on fighting racism and advancing basic human rights and equity for Black people.

Chaos Theory: A field of study within mathematics which looks at systems in states of apparent disorder and investigates how small changes may affect their outcome.

Coherent: Orderly and harmonious synchronization of systems. In this chapter, it refers to a coherent connection between the heart and the brain from which we are more easily able to regulate our emotions and reactions.

Diversity: The influences, experiences, and education that create our unique perspectives in the world. Any of these differences make-up who we are, including but not limited to: gender, race/ethnicity, generation, sexual orientation, religion, ability, veteran status, where we grew up, family status, education, etc.

Equity: Fair treatment within the context of need. Equality is treating people *the same*, whereas equity is treating people according to the specific circumstances of their situation.

Exclusion: Intentionally or unintentionally ignoring or mistreating a person or group of people based on their personal diversity characteristics.

Inclusion: Connecting people in an environment of respect, regardless of their differences. Giving equal access and opportunity to all people and removing barriers for those groups who have been historically or systemically discriminated against.

Meet Brilliant Practicing Expert™ Susan McCuistion:

Speaker | Facilitator | Coach | #1 Bestselling Author

Susan McCuistion is a cultural practitioner and creator of Compassionate Diversity®, which integrates concepts from the fields of intercultural communication, emotional intelligence, leadership, science, and more, into powerful tools for change. Foundational to Compassionate Diversity® is *The Resilience Profitability Process*™, which incorporates three interrelated concepts - Comprehension, Connection, and Collaboration - to build resilience and inclusion in organizations and our world.

SUSAN'S SPECIAL INVITATION FOR YOU:
Join Susan's free, self-guided, 7-day challenge to learn more about how the 7 Principles of Compassionate Diversity® can help you build the foundation necessary to comprehend, connect, and collaborate in more compassionate ways.

Go to: https://www.susanmccuistion.com/cd7daychallenge

Business: daiOne, LLC

Even if you're committ ed to diversity, you're probably sti ll struggling to understand how it aff ects your business, and you're not alone. Fostering collaborati on, making full use of technology, and engaging employees are challenging businesses across industries. Additionally, when diversity is not managed well, you will miss opportunities and lose employees.

Diversity is unavoidable. Inclusion is a choice. Inclusion is about much more than just "everyone's welcome." It's about leading with compassion, a skill that can be taught. When consistently implemented, compassion positively affects morale, recruiting, retention, and your bottom line. After working with Susan, you will be prepared and empowered to lead through compassion and achieve greater success because of it.

Website: https://www.susanmccuistion.com/

Connect with Susan on these social accounts:
LinkedIn: https://www.linkedin.com/in/susanmccuistion
Twitter: https://twitter.com/SusanMcCuistion
Facebook: https://www.facebook.com/SusanMcCuistion
Author Profile: amazon.com/author/susanmccuistion

Download Mobile App: BrilliantBizBook from your App Store. It contains everything related to this Book Series and its Authors.

Allow Me to Introduce Brilliant Practicing Expert™
Shalini Nag, Ph.D., by Maggie Mongan

Shalini and I were introduced to one another via a mutual friend, Mike Raber. Shalini had just relocated to the Milwaukee area. She was quiet, light-hearted, and beamed with warmth. Shortly after we met, it was evident Shalini had some great wisdom to share.

I posed a couple of questions to Shalini and she opened up and told me what she knew and why she knew what she did about business. She was practical, had great depth, and my attention. Shalini was referencing uncommon knowledge and being the scholar she is, she validated her comments. I appreciate this approach.

Over time our conversations were getting deeper and Shalini shared how she wants to change the world, which I'm sure we'll discuss in one of her podcast episodes.

Shalini has beautiful insights into people, as well as organizational and cultural development. Just like big business, small business has a culture, which is the underlying tone of the business. This is commonly experienced through communications or conversations, which have a significant impact on how your people feel and perform. Listen to the master who can help you have better conversations and fortify your people's performance. Also, remember to engage further with her offer at the bottom of her author's page.

Flip the Paradigm:
Embrace the Human Approach
to Boost Your Business

by Shalini Nag, Ph.D.

The Heart of the Matter

"Great companies are built on robust strategies that encompass their finances, operations, products, and customers. Exceptional companies that remain sustainable, innovative, and relevant in an ever-shifting, evolving world are those that focus as earnestly on their people as on their strategy."[1]

We are living in times of extraordinary change, unprecedented uncertainty, and yet, an unparalleled opportunity for small businesses. Small Business Owners (SBOs) who are ready to overcome their fears, embrace innovation, and break away from "how things have always been done," will be uniquely positioned to leapfrog ahead of their competitors.

In some ways, a small business is better prepared to navigate fast-moving, dynamic environments than corporations because of customer-proximity and agility-friendly size. However, the SBO, bombarded by innumerable tools to carry out each task, overwhelmed by the frequency, magnitude and number of decisions and tasks on hand, is susceptible to the pitfall of deprioritizing their people and culture.

Overlooking people can prove expensive; it is detrimental to business growth because, irrespective of industry, product, or service offering, "Culture is a company's greatest intangible asset."[2] From Zappos to Southwest Airlines, Zoom Video Communications to ADP[3,4], the contribution of culture to their success is undeniable.

"The pace of change is disrupting businesses right and left. The plan - organize - command - control model of leadership can no longer deliver the results we need."[5]

Furthermore, annual studies of 6000 organizations, representing 10 million employees in 80 countries, resulting in Fortune's 100 Best Companies to Work for list, demonstrate that great cultures allow organizations to attract and retain the best talent, innovate faster, have higher customer satisfaction, and achieve better financial performance.[6]

What do leaders of successful organizations know? It's their people who drive business success and are, therefore, placed squarely at the heart of their strategy.

The Success Delta™: People at the Heart of Your Organization

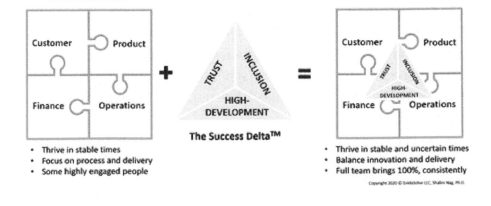

The Success Delta™

Numerous global studies, conducted through the years[7,8,9,10], have discovered the crucial quality that makes a company exceptional.

Employees at exceptional companies bring their discretionary effort to work and drive extraordinary results.

Indeed, these are the kind of businesses where, when a pandemic makes live, in-person training impossible, the team comes together to reinvent their services, relaunch them, and obtain client buy-in[11], all within 48 hours.

You may ask, "Why do their employees go above and beyond consistently?"

The difference is *The Success Delta*™—3 core elements of adaptable, high-performance organizations that thrive despite dynamic external trends and crises: Trust, Inclusion, and High-development.

Trust: It is probably no surprise how trust between leaders, managers, and employees gives each individual the feeling they belong and the confidence that their team has their back. An environment of trust creates the psychological safety that reduces silence[12] so employees proactively highlight issues and resolve them before they have a negative, long-term impact on the business.

What may be surprising is the magnitude of impact—employees who feel heard are nearly 5 times more likely to perform their best work![13]

Inclusion: As an SBO, you might believe that inclusion doesn't apply to you[14], especially if you've always hired locally. But you'd be mistaken. Even before a pandemic and unrest about discrimination at work in 2020 changed the workplace forever, the workforce was becoming progressively diverse.

Increasingly, leaders must manage employees who differ not just in visible characteristics such as race, ethnicity, and gender, but also by generation, thinking and working styles, education, and digital comfort.

Diversity increases return on equity by nearly 53% and profit margins by 14%[15], but only when an inclusive workplace augments voice[12]—the uninhibited sharing of employees' unique strengths, perspectives, and ideas. Inclusion is key to enabling your business to constantly innovate, evolve, and overcome challenges, no matter the business size.

High-development: "There just isn't enough talent!" "I don't know why they won't just do what needs to be done."

If this sounds familiar, you have experience with a low-development mindset. Oddly, low-development mindsets frequently appear alongside expectations of high-performance, which are rarely met.

In contrast, when leaders create a high-development environment, they focus on enhancing employees' skills and abilities, so they can take on bigger roles and contribute more, while automatically generating goodwill and loyalty.

By embracing *The Success Delta*™, leaders are rewarded with loyal, high-performance teams, who drive business outcomes beyond expectation.

The Human Approach to The Success Delta™

When faced with declining employee engagement and productivity, and increased turnover or workplace conflict, desperate for a quick solution, leaders often resort to purchasing the shiniest tool promising to be a panacea. Unfortunately, these point solutions target a single superficial symptom and not the root cause, so issues continue to recur.

Therefore, despite widespread deployment of employee surveys, rewards management, and learning systems, employee engagement has stagnated, with only 6 - 17% of workers fully engaged worldwide.[8]

What's more concerning for the SBO is these numbers vary little irrespective of company size![16] So, no matter where you're located or how many employees you have, you may be missing 80-95% of the discretionary effort of your people!

"As Chief Financial Officer, you have a fiduciary responsibility for culture—you cannot ignore the hidden costs of disengagement."[16]

It's unbelievable that any leader would willingly accept such poor performance from any other asset!

It is, therefore, a fair deduction that the leaders of those 84% of disengaged employees are likely unaware of:

a. The impact to business—an excuse that you, the reader, no longer have

b. *The Success Delta*™—knowledge that you, the reader, are now privy to

c. How to embed The Success Delta™ in your business—read on!

In the bygone industrial age, companies competed on efficiency. To win, they focused on process optimization, automation, and cost reduction. Then began the transition to *The Next Age*™.[17] As computer technology advanced, collecting overwhelming amounts of data became possible. Analytical thinking, equations, and digital tools took center stage.

Today, computers are often better equipped than people to gather, store, and analyze information. While insight and innovation remain within the human purview, given this history, it is perhaps understandable why a leader may turn to shiny tools to resolve their people concerns.

However, contrary to obvious assumptions, embedding *The Success Delta*™ into your business is not dependent on massive financial investments or sophisticated tools.

Instead, it is achieved by flipping the paradigm and investing the time and energy in *Conversations for Business Success*™: *the right conversations with the right people, at the right time, in the right manner.*

The 4 Dimensions of Conversations for Business Success™

Seem simple? It is!!

Conversations are at the core of human interaction, learning, and evolution. Just as people are at the heart of a business, so conversation is the life-blood driving business success.

Think back to a pivotal moment—when you felt heard and valued, when you were motivated to go above and beyond!

Now, answer this—did human connection and conversation play a role?

REMEMBER: "Becoming a great leader takes time, self-awareness, humility, and a willingness to learn. First and foremost, be a good human—encourage others, look for strengths, and create an environment where everyone can excel."[18]

Begin your journey with *The 4 Dimensions of Conversations for Business Success*™.

1: Have the right conversations

When you hear "conversation" do you suppress a shudder and think, "More conversation? Don't we have enough meetings? When do I get work done?"

You're NOT alone! It isn't fun for anyone when the day is coming to an end, you're exhausted from endless meetings or sales calls, and your to-do list has grown longer than you started with!

The solution? Not more conversations but, instead, the right conversations.

The world of work can be categorized into innovation (e.g., product development), driving (e.g., sales), stabilization (e.g., establishing best practices), and development (e.g., hiring and training). The business outcomes you desire must drive the type of work you engage in, and consequently, the conversations you have.

You know you're having the right conversations if:

- Each conversation helps you achieve a key business outcome, and
- You maintain a balance between conversations in each category—innovation, driving, stabilization, and development.

2: The right people

Experienced this? You're in a meeting and have no idea why; neither your presence nor opinion seems desired; yet, you're stuck, waiting for it to be over.

Don't let that happen to your people. The right conversations have specific goals. If someone isn't an active contributor, decision-maker, or driver, they shouldn't be in it!

3: The right time

Most SBOs feel like they are constantly drinking from a fire hose. They move from crisis to crisis, from one immediate priority to the next. Conversations become reactive—and you're playing catch up instead of playing to win.

When you shift to proactive conversations, you get ahead of issues. You plan ahead, put in guardrails, create Plan B. Fires are doused when the first spark appears. The fire hose becomes redundant and stress becomes a distant memory.

Making the shift to proactive conversations takes time and effort upfront, but yields consistent, ongoing returns in saved time, happier teams, higher productivity, and sales.

4: The right manner

Finally, consider the quality of the conversation. "The type of conversation you have with the people around you has a profound impact on your experiences, relationships, and accomplishments."[19] In simple terms, the higher the quality of your conversations, the better the outcomes you generate.

$$\text{Conversational Quality} \propto \text{Outcomes Quality}$$

There are two primary levers to enhance the quality of a conversation—Direction and Tone.

Direction—Who's doing the talking?

Do you remember that all-staff meeting where you presented the business results, ran overtime, and skipped Q&A?

Have you wondered, "I tell them what to do but they just don't get it!"

If these situations seem familiar, you might be talking *at* your people instead of *with* them. Don't get me wrong—one-way communication has its role. Sometimes the right conversation is aimed at sharing information—a discourse, an article, or a memo may be exactly what's needed.

However, if one-way communication is your default, it's no wonder that your people don't get it! Unless they are actively contributing, your audience pays attention for less than a minute before tuning you out![20]

More importantly, you're missing out on 80% of your organization's potential for improvement.[21]

Tone—How does it make you feel?

Think back once more to your pivotal moment. Recall feeling heard, valued, and motivated. This is how you want your people to feel whenever they engage in conversation at work.

In other words, the best conversations are generative. They are:

- Appreciative—add value by sharing knowledge, creating insights, and developing new solutions.
- Inquiry-based—driven by questions originating in genuine curiosity.
- Multiplicative—yield greater outcomes than otherwise possible.

Generative conversations enhance collaboration, expand awareness, spark innovation, and inspire superlative work.

"Leadership lives in the relationship between those who lead and those who follow. If you're going to grow that relationship you have to be interested in the people you are leading. Then you begin to welcome differences."[22]

At this point, you might think, "This is great for a brainstorming session, but how about situations where we need improved processes or team performance?"

That's when a strengths-based approach can transform an uncomfortable, demotivating conversation into a generative one. Begin by asking the following questions:

- What are the unique characteristics (potential, strengths, and capabilities)?
- Where is the desire and opportunity for growth?
- How can existing strengths be applied to further the desired growth?

By starting from a position of strength, applying appreciative inquiry[23], and establishing the desired outcome, the conversation becomes collaborative and generative.

The strengths-based approach can exponentially amplify business success. By perfecting natural strengths, you can quickly create a team of superstars, whereas the same investment focused on weaknesses would, at best, yield above-average performance.

Strength	=	Talent	X	Investment
(Ability to consistently provide near-perfect performance)		(Natural behavioral styles)		(Time spent building skills & knowledge, practicing)

"What if," you may wonder, inspired by the possibilities, "we haven't been having the right quality of conversations yet? What if we frequently have destructive conflict? Is there a solution?"

"When we resort to judgment and blame, that's when we begin to lose ourselves."[24]

Breathe a sigh of relief, because *ALLIES@Work*™ offers 6 steps to minimize conflict. With *ALLIES@Work*™, you can step away from judgment towards human connection and collaboration.

1. **A**ccept that you have blind spots.

2. **L**isten to prove them right.

3. **L**earn with curiosity.

4. **I**nvestigate possibilities.

5. **E**xamine your frame of reference.

6. **S**ynthesize and share.

Transform your conversations. Elevate your business.
"2020 has been a year of turmoil and change, but for forward-thinking SBOs, this is an amazing time to rethink strategies and develop solid cultural foundations, no matter if their businesses are thriving or challenged."[25]

If business is slow, you have the unique opportunity to use the downtime to set up your business to thrive. If instead, business is in high-growth mode, it is imperative that you attend to your company's culture now, to preempt issues of burnout, low productivity, high turnover, and consequential financial underperformance in the future.

Amidst a global pandemic, we've each come to realize the value of human connection in our lives. By taking the human approach of *Conversations for Business Success*™, you can leave outdated command-and-control management behind, harness the discretionary effort of your team, and lead your business confidently into the future.

Flip the Paradigm: Embrace the Human Approach to Boost Your Business
Glossary:

Agility-friendly size: small enough to change quickly and easily when needed, through frequent reassessment and adaptation of plans.

Appreciative: creating, adding, or otherwise increasing the value.

Appreciative Inquiry: a conversational methodology that uses questions aimed at adding value to drive results.

ALLIES@Work™: a 6-step conversational framework that effectively minimizes conflict in the workplace.

Conversations for Business Success™: a 4-dimensional, human approach to embedding The Success Delta™ – trust, inclusion, high-development – within a business, and driving business results.

Culture: the underlying beliefs, assumptions, values, and behaviors that contribute to the unique social and psychological environment of an organization.

Customer-proximity: closeness to the customer due to fewer degrees of separation between decision-makers and those who directly serve the customer.

Digital comfort: state of ease with digital tools, platforms, and mindsets.

Direction: whether a conversation is one-way, two-way, or multi-way.

Discretionary effort: the additional thinking and effort people could give if they were motivated to, above and beyond average expectations, or stated requirements.

Exceptional companies: companies that deliver extraordinary financial results due to their ability to tap into the discretionary effort of their people.

Generative conversation: conversations that add value, are driven by curiosity, and yield specific outcomes.

High-development: values and therefore emphasizes continuous personal and professional growth, resulting in ongoing improvement in performance.

High-performance: faster, more efficient, or otherwise better performance than the norm.

Inclusion: where the inherent worth, dignity, and uniqueness of each individual is recognized, valued, and sought after.

Inquiry-based: a conversational approach that utilizes questions stemming from curiosity with the aim to generate better understanding.

Low-development mindset: an attitude that undervalues personal and professional growth and, therefore, avoids investing time, energy, or resources in the same.

Multiplicative: increasing value significantly through multiplication rather than addition.

Point solutions: isolated solutions that target a specific symptom instead of resolving the whole, underlying problem.

Psychological safety: feeling accepted and respected and therefore, being able to show and employ one's authentic self without fear of negative consequences to self-image, status, or career.

Silence: the extent to which or how often a person intentionally withholds ideas or issues, often due to a fear of negative consequences.

Strengths-based: focused on recognizing and growing the inherent strengths of individuals with the aim of deploying a team of individuals with complementary strengths.

The Success Delta™: a people strategy model, encompassing trust, inclusion, and high-development, that unleashes the discretionary effort of employees and sets exceptional organizations apart.

Tone: how a conversation makes the participants feel.

Trust: belief in the reliability, ability, truth, and strength of a person, manager, or an organization's leadership team.

Voice: the extent to which or how often a person speaks up with constructive ideas or issues at work.

Meet Brilliant Practicing Expert™ Shalini Nag, Ph.D.:

People Strategist | Consultant | Trainer | Speaker

A global citizen and avid traveler, Dr. Shalini Nag is a firm believer in the limitless potential of people united by a common goal. She has experienced this first-hand in her work with over 85 organizations worldwide.

Shalini leans on her scientific background and natural empathy to blend data-driven approaches with real-world business know-how. She aligns culture with strategy to shift organizations from reactive problem-solving to proactive issue prevention. Her versatile and innovative solutions equip business leaders to embed *The Success Delta*™ in their organizations – breaking down barriers and building extraordinary teams who deliver exceptional results.

SHALINI'S SPECIAL INVITATION FOR YOU:

Begin your journey to embedding *The Success Delta*™ in your organization with this free guide on implementing ALLIES@Work™.

Click here: https://www.evidasolve.com/brilliant

Business: EvidaSolve LLC

EvidaSolve transforms businesses into Thriving Talent Magnets™ – exceptional organizations where the best seek to work, and employees become life-long advocates – through innovative, data-driven approaches.

EvidaSolve provides small and mid-size companies with versatile people strategy consulting to create a competitive edge that propels business growth in both stable and dynamic environments. Additionally, keynote speeches and innovative training programs transform your leaders, mobilize your teams, reduce conflict, and maximize performance to create measurable results.

Bottom line: If your organization is constantly growing, evolving, or changing, and you are striving to generate sustainable outcomes, EvidaSolve can help you harness the power of your people and surpass the perceived potential of your business.

Website: https://www.evidasolve.com

Connect with Shalini on these social accounts:
LinkedIn: https://www.linkedin.com/in/dr-shalini-nag-talent-advisor
Facebook: https://www.facebook.com/EvidaSolve.Talent.Strategy

Download Mobile App: BrilliantBizBook from your App Store.
It contains everything related to this Book Series and its Authors.

PERFORMANCE

PILLAR 3

PRODUCTIVITY

Allow Me to Introduce Brilliant Practicing Expert™

Mike Raber, by Maggie Mongan

To our readers, Mike Raber isn't a new expert to our *Community of Brilliant Practicing Experts*™, as he's written insightful chapters in Volumes 1 and 2. He's back one last time to share a personally vulnerable story with you. Why? It was a powerful *a-ha* for him, and research reveals it most likely will be for you too.

I've previously introduced Mike as a wicked-smart nonconformist, a strong and gentle leader, and masterful at connecting people. Mike is highly accomplished. So what's the issue? As accomplished as Mike was, he didn't believe he was.

During this chapter, Mike reveals how he, himself, was impeding upon his success. I commend Mike for revealing this truth with our readers! He told me how important it was "for no one else to suffer needlessly."

Take this opportunity to meet and explore your own Imposter Syndrome, which is activated when circumstances trigger it - regardless of how accomplished you may be. This implies you, Small Business Owner, are constantly susceptible to your Imposter overruling your truth. Be sure to engage with Mike's special offer at the bottom of his author's page to learn more and improve your business's productivity.

Are Your Influencer Capabilities Being Overpowered by Imposter Syndrome?

by Mike Raber

Did you know the majority of small business owners aren't aware their imposter syndrome holds them back from succeeding? I know this firsthand. I'd like to introduce you to *The 4 Secrets to Overcoming Imposter Syndrome*™.

Secret #1 – Own your expertise, don't fall prey to your insecurities!

Have you ever found yourself stepping into an opportunity excited and ready to do something amazing? Then, just as you are about to leap, you hear that nagging little voice: "Who, you? Are you serious? You're not *good enough*. You just need to practice a little more." or even, "Sure, that person may be able to do that, but not you!"

For many years I was this person. I'd wake up with a vision and had planned all the great things I was going to do that day only to psych myself out by the time I finished breakfast. I had all the resources I needed to accomplish great things; yet, I never believed I was truly ready, would be *good enough,* or that I knew enough. Even though, throughout my life, I had taken on and accomplished many great challenges.

I was always the guy who would step forward and say, "Yes, I will help you." I owned and ran many successful businesses over the years; yet, I still never believed I had sufficient skills. I lived with an overwhelming fear of imposter syndrome: "a sense I was a professional phony." This belief was consistent and constant, even as I prepared myself to become an influencer.

I always had a nagging feeling there was still one more book I needed to read or one more seminar I had to attend. No matter how much I learned about a topic, it still didn't feel like it was enough. If I put on a seminar or found a coaching client, I wasn't ready to be the guy. I would be an imposter.

It wasn't until I realized true expertise comes from taking what we learn and applying it to real-life that I started to believe I was *the guy*.

Granted, I may not have been a validated expert; yet, I certainly knew more than most. Many may argue that an expert is someone who knows just a little more than the person in front of them and isn't afraid to take the lead. Over time, the title *Expert* begins to attach itself to the leader. What if I told you, "Congratulations, you're already an expert!" even though no one may have given you this title?

I'm going to begin by sharing how I went from imposter to influencer. Are you thinking, "What do you mean by imposter?"

The Miriam-Webster Dictionary defines imposter syndrome as, "a psychological condition that is characterized by persistent doubt concerning one's abilities or accomplishments accompanied by the fear of being exposed as a fraud despite evidence of one's ongoing success."[1]

Imposter syndrome is a pattern of thinking which affects the way you see yourself. It can be associated with low self-esteem or a fear of not being *good enough*.

When someone has imposter syndrome, they often live in constant fear of being called out as an imposter—falsely believing somehow people will discover they're really a fraud, even though they truly are an expert.

"I spent my entire twenty-year career at Microsoft hoping not to be *found out* and after retiring my first thought was, I can't believe I got away with it."[2]

This fear has no basis in reality; yet, the threat can still feel real. Both men and women can be influenced by feeling like a *poseur*. The idea of only succeeding due to luck, and not because of your talent or qualifications, was first identified in 1978 by psychologists Pauline Rose Clance and Suzanne Imes. In their paper, they theorized women were uniquely affected by imposter syndrome. They tend to experience it more intensely and are more limited by it. It became widely known as imposter syndrome in subsequent years.

What if I told you the world needs you to share what you already have? It's true. The mere fact that you're reading this book demonstrates you're already on your own path to personal and professional growth.

It's time to own your truth and show up as the expert you are. Don't let the fear of not being *good enough* stop you! "Learn to say "yes" to every opportunity, even if you don't know how to do it. If you're seen as the person who always says "yes," more opportunities will be presented to you. If you step into a new opportunity and don't know how to do it, learn it quickly, then surround yourself with people who know more than you do."[3]

The number one fear I have is flying; yet, I'm sitting on an airplane writing this on my way to the eWomenNetwork Platinum Summit designed for women professionals and business owners who have a goal to earn one million dollars and more in their businesses. I was extremely nervous about registering for the event, as I was sure I'd be one of the few men attending. I knew I may be the unicorn in the room; however, I believed I needed to be there.

Do you often find yourself having high aspirations yet feeling like somehow you don't fit in?

A week before the Summit, I attended a networking meeting that consisted of 12 women. The meeting started with everyone introducing themselves and sharing a challenge they were experiencing. One person's challenge was how she had two small children and was trying to build her business around taking care of them.

As each woman spoke, it became obvious to me why 98% of my clients were female professionals and business owners. I, too, was the primary caregiver of three small children while building three businesses. Fortunately, all three kids survived; however, two of the businesses died a horrible death. The healthy business survived, and I sold it profitably later.

My own superpower was learning how to step into the role of primary caregiver to three incredible kids. Additionally, while helping my wife build her successful business, I was building and scaling different businesses of my own.

While working with clients I would often share many lessons learned via fun stories through books, podcasts, and training programs. Superpower Alert: Share a complex challenge with me and I'll give you the solution through a simple, easy-to-grasp story.

Granted, I had my own insecurities about whether or not I belonged at the Summit. I thought that if by attending and expanding my network, I could touch just one heart, who am I to let fear stop me?

What goals have you accomplished by pushing past fear? Did you push past them because the thought of *not* accomplishing your goal was far worse than the fear itself?

Let us journey back to exploring imposter syndrome.

Secret #2 – Whether or not you're an imposter, expert, or influencer, lies in your belief about yourself!

"Beware of the thief on the street that's after your purse. But also, beware of the thief in your mind that's after your promise."[4]

Years ago, I ran a limousine company and my operating expenses were twice as much as my incoming revenue. Then, I started a real estate firm and bought a chauffeur training school—all while raising my kids. I additionally hired a business coach and worked with him for seven years. I read approximately one hundred books and listened to two hundred different cassettes and CD programs on business and personal growth. Over those seven years, I was able to scale the limousine company, and profitably sold it. I was able to pay off a lot of debt and move my family back to my hometown in Wisconsin.

I should have been on top of the world; yet, I still didn't think I knew enough. Then I became Director of Training for ReMax and achieved ten different real estate certifications in two years. I still didn't think I knew enough. So, I left ReMax and became a financial adviser. I wrote two books and became part of the *Brilliant Breakthroughs for the Small Business Owner* book series, and became a #1 Bestselling Business Author. Somehow, I still didn't feel like I knew enough!

Are you starting to see an ongoing theme of imposter syndrome? The underlying question became—did I truly *not* know enough, or did I *not* deserve the rewards and financial benefits which give credence to someone with expert status?

Hindsight: I had two underlying faulty beliefs. My greatest false belief, and by far the most dangerous of them all, was the idea that "money was bad!" And I also believed that I should help people for a nominal fee. Then I would be able to serve more people as it was the "right thing to do." Thus, I found myself charging way less than

I should, instead of charging what my services were truly worth. I was often frustrated because, without adequate funds, I wasn't able to achieve my goals. My turning point came once I truly believed money was a tool; I then recognized I needed more money to help more people. This simple mindset shift radically turned around my business.

The second false belief was revealed to me a few years back by a master coach. He asked me, "What would happen if your business failed?" My face lit up as I replied, "If my business completely failed, I would drive a semi-truck." Don't laugh—it was a dream of mine since childhood.

Laughing, he replied, "Bad news, you're more excited about your Plan B than the success of your business. It's no wonder you keep hitting a glass ceiling!"

Even though I worked with various business coaches over the past 20 years and my knowledge about business continued to soar, my business finances continued to crash. None of the coaches, books, CD programs, or seminars touched on my true underlying challenge—my belief about money.

It wasn't until I had my back pushed up against the wall and started exploring all of who I was, what my own superpowers were, and my purpose for being here, that my truth was revealed.

No matter how much I thought I needed to learn, ultimately, the biggest challenges I needed to overcome were: the belief that making a lot of money or building a fortune was bad; I needed to give up my passion to serve my purpose; and, I still needed to learn just one more thing and maybe then I would be an expert in the core areas I tied to my vision and my purpose. Only then, I believed, would the world come and say, "We have been waiting for you to arrive; please help us. We will happily hire you or become part of your community." Talk about a crock of BS I was telling myself. Clearly, I was delusional. Do you find yourself doing this too?

Secret #3 – What your mind can believe, through proper conditioning, you can achieve.

Henry Ford stated, "Whether you think you can, or you think you can't, either way, you're right."[5]

According to Miriam-Webster, the definition of influencer is, "One who exerts influence: a person who inspires or guides the actions of others."[6]

First: wealth, in the hands of the right person or organization, can yield amazing results. Second: we are all experts at something.

A one-year-old looks up to the three-year-old who can easily walk across the room. The toddler realizes the trick to walking is just taking one step after another and begins to walk until he is able to run.

The beginning musician looks up to the music teacher, who can easily explain the different scales or notes. The musician, who, after practicing her scales, then plays a piece that excites the birds in a neighboring tree. It stems back to the difference between the beginner, imposter, and expert mindset.

In the areas of my specialization, I am an expert in my craft. Compared to some, you are an expert in your craft. Together, we can make amazing things happen. Imagine a world where we are all sharing our expertise and work together to lift up one another.

Secret #4 – Be coachable and trust your mentors or guides!

I have found that greatness comes from the absence of fear or doubt. First, your mind must see and believe your desired target is easily attainable. Then, your body or muscle memory will follow.

I remember when my daughter, Sabrina, was 8. She wanted to join a club basketball team. The tryouts involved having to shoot three free throws in a row. Never having shot a free throw before, Sabrina was panicking. I told her to relax and we would go to the gym, where I'd teach her how to successfully make all three free throws.

We went to the gym. I told her to take the ball, go to the free-throw line, and look at the hoop. Then, move forward while looking at the hoop until she reached the point where I knew she could easily make the shot. Standing there holding the ball, I told her to make the shot. Swoosh! The ball went right in. I handed Sabrina the ball and had her back up to the free-throw line. I told her: "Look at the hoop, close your eyes, and hold the ball. Now, visualize taking one hundred shots easily making every single one." We then went home.

The next day we went to her tryouts. Sabrina walked up to the free-throw line and I told her, "Close your eyes and once again visualize making the shot." As she opened her eyes, I told her to release and shoot the ball just like she did the previous one hundred times. Leaving her hands, the ball went up and swoosh right into the hoop. She made all three shots.

When tryouts were finished, the coach asked me if Sabrina practiced shooting free throws a lot. Smiling, I replied, "Nope, that was her first time." Coach inquired, "But how did she make all three? She was the only one who did." I replied, "Simple, she didn't know that she couldn't."

Yes, Sabrina made the team and had a great season. The question is: Was Sabrina an expert at shooting free throws? Hardly. She missed many free throws after that day. However, in that particular moment, making the free throw was all her muscle memory knew.

Remember this influencer ...

I would argue that being an expert is about having the proper mindset wired for favorable outcomes AND being skilled to support such outcomes.

When all else fails, default to Aristotle's wisdom, "Men acquire a particular quality by constantly acting a certain way."[7]

Many say, "Fake it until you make it." I have found this encourages the imposter syndrome. I would rather contend that it should be, "Faith it until you become it." It first comes from the belief that it's possible, even if you haven't done it yet.

Are Your Influencer Capabilities Being Overpowered by Imposter Syndrome?
Glossary:

Coachable: Being accountable and willing to learn from a coach or mentor.

Delusional: When a person cannot tell what is real from what is imagined. The main feature of this disorder is the presence of delusions, which are unshakable beliefs in something untrue.

Expert: Having, involving, or displaying special skill or knowledge derived from training or experience.

Glass Ceiling: Invisible or mental barrier through which the next stage or level of advancement can be seen, but not reached due to limiting beliefs, mental blocks, or low self-esteem.

Imposter: One who assumes false identity or title for the purpose of deception.

Influencer: One who exerts influence; a person who inspires or guides the actions of others.

Imposter Syndrome: Psychological condition characterized by persistent doubt concerning one's abilities or accomplishments accompanied by the fear of being exposed as a fraud, despite evidence of one's ongoing success.

Insecurities: Deficient in self-assurance: beset by fear and anxiety. Not believing one has the competence to do something well.

Fraud/Phony: Not genuine or real, such as intended to deceive or mislead.

Platinum Summit: Conference for professionals holding an eWomenNetwork Platinum level membership.

Poseur: A person who pretends to be what he or she is not or insincere person.

Profitability: State or condition of yielding a financial profit or gain.

Psyche myself out: Convincing myself I'm not ready nor able to do something I want to do.

Scale: Having the ability to grow without hinderance

Superpower: Unique skill or ability, which allows us to step into our purpose.

Unicorn: Something unusual, rare, or unique.

Visualize: To see or form a mental image of a goal or desired outcome.

Meet Brilliant Practicing Expert™ Mike Raber:

2-Time Bestselling Business Author | Speaker
Trainer | Small Business Coach

Mike's skills and capabilities of leadership, building relationships, growing different businesses, and writing a book with his daughter on the *secret to raising financially savvy kids* have evolved to make him the father, business, and wealth architect he is today.

Mike is continually perfecting his skills in the areas of financial management, leadership, sales training, and business development. Perhaps even more amazing is how Mike has applied these to building an impressive and strong professional network through his unique relationship-building techniques.

MIKE'S SPECIAL INVITATION FOR YOU:

To learn *The 4 Secrets to Overcoming Imposter Syndrome*™

Go to: https://www.microbizcorp.com/the-influencers-journey

Business: 100 Million Strong, SPC

Mike has lived boldly in some extreme situations, which has assisted him in refining his approach to people and success. He created the influencer's journey, a collection of lessons from different influencers working together to build a movement of 100 million people poised to positively bring peace and improve the community around them.

Mike works with coaches, influencers, and professionals who are striving to be thought leaders. He helps them fully understand their own superpowers and fulfill their mission. Mike created a powerful framework to help his clients remove false beliefs, that often get in their way, such as, dealing with imposter syndrome and the many challenges faced by small business owners.

Website Address: www.theinfluencersjourney.com

Connect with Mike on these social accounts:
Facebook:
https://www.facebook.com/The-Influencers-Journey-100573648445334
Instagram: https://www.instagram.com/mraber20/
Twitter: https://twitter.com/Theinfl78777828
YouTube: https://bit.ly/3gC5uMB
Author Profile: http://www.amazon.com/author/mikeraber

Download Mobile App: BrilliantBizBook from your App Store.
It contains everything related to this Book Series and its Authors.

Allow Me to Introduce Brilliant Practicing Expert™
Dennis Hill, Ph.D., by Maggie Mongan

Simply stated, proximity brought Dennis Hill and our book series together several years ago. Dennis appreciated our community's commitment to supporting the underserved Small Business Sector and immediately offered his business's workspace for our in-person training and release day events – and he's doing it again.

I'm happy to formally introduce Dr. Dennis Hill, a *Brilliant Practicing Expert*™, who pens his wisdom to support your performance of productivity and profitability.

Dennis is a tenured expert who wishes to make the intersection of life, business, and technology seamless. His passion to help business leaders and owners support their businesses with power-packed; yet simplified technology, is undeniable. Consistently throughout the decades, Dennis is globally recognized for his foresight and commitment to assure big tech and the government honor the sanctity of people owning their data.

Small Business Owners need to streamline productivity, which ultimately increases profitability. Dennis wrote to help you understand the gap of what typically happens with business operations and the possibilities of better solutions. Your tech stack doesn't need to be complicated, nor expensive. He reveals a practical solution to help you improve your support activities for your operations. Remember to engage with his offer at the bottom of his author's page – it was designed to boost your productivity and profit.

Integrate for Well-Managed, Intentional Growth

by Dennis Hill, Ph.D.

Small and Mid-size Businesses Make Brilliant Breakthroughs

We are living in the Fourth Industrial Revolution. Are you surprised? You're a big part of the current revolution. Disruptions occur daily across the globe. Their impact on business-to-business (B2B) and business-to-consumer (B2C) relationships manifest locally.[1] Crop fires in coffee-producing nations directly affect the corner coffee shop just as it affects a global chain of stores. Strikes in Asia or a worldwide pandemic can delay delivery of inventory to your business, the same as *Big-Box* stores.

In the digital world, laws on other continents, like the General Data Protection Act in the European Union, have been felt by every business which has a website.[2] Global communication has become as easy as opening an app on the phone, and information on the world wide web is doubling as fast as every 12 hours,[3] which begs the question, "Can you, your employees, your business, and your systems handle it all?" Have you succumbed to an excess of activities distracting you from your business?

Small Business is Ground Zero of Every Industrial Revolution

The first industrial revolution began around the mid-18th century when machine-based manufacturing using water and steam replaced hand manufacturing. The second revolution, marked by electric power, created mass production lines. The third, according to the World Economic Forum (WEF), employed electronics and information technology to automate manufacturing. Just as the second scaled the first, the fourth industrial revolution extends the third revolution to a new age of knowledge creation at unprecedented speeds and disrupting trajectories.[3]

Examining the evolution and formalization of business in all respects, only small and mid-size companies (SMBs) have sustainably and consistently provided the platform for innovation and experimentation across every revolutionary period. According to the North American Industry Classification System (NAICS), the vast majority of companies in the USA, about 15.5 million of 17.3 million, employ fewer than 100 employees. Of those, 12.1 million employs just 1 to 4 people. Clearly, people express passion and creativity in start-ups and small companies that embody brilliant breakthroughs.[4]

Paradigms that Turn on a Dime

Every owner shares the same desire for success but is compelled to become a *pseudo-expert* in many other areas. Today's owner understands product development, manufacturing, lead generation, marketing, human resources, accounting, business law, and even closing sales. They all apply or will apply to run the business.[5]

Fundamentally, employees bring their knowledge and time to a job.[6] A deficit in one demands an excess of the other. To have a shortage of both time and experience is equivalent to boarding an already sinking ship. Benjamin Franklin reminded his readers that "time is money" in his essay entitled "Advice to a Young Tradesman."[7] We must learn to manage both with laser-focus and sagacious intent, and this means efficiently acquiring, maintaining, and leveraging information while overcoming the limits of time and experience. Only then can we expect to manage our business for well-managed, intentional growth.

Isolated, Interfaced, or Integrated?

With a robust accounting system in hand, like Intuit's QuickBooks, Microsoft's Dynamics, or one of many others on the market,[8] business owners are left to redirect valuable innovation and experimentation time from products and services or engaging prospects and customers in profitable relationships, to building operating infrastructures without tools. Most owners start with paper-based systems, with programs for email, spreadsheets, and word processing.[9] Based on a belief that *there's a program for this or an app for that*, the owner will spend countless hours learning about software. One can only imagine the years required to learn marketing, e-commerce, workforce recruitment, prospecting, customer relations, human resource administration, employment law, and a plethora of other functions.[10]

Faced with so many software options and a finite amount of time, most owners resign and take a wait-and-see approach when it comes to technology, perpetuating manual processes, like a pencil, paper, and sticky notes, to get an order. No company is scalable, let alone sustainable, that uses manual methods in this century.[6]

There are three ways to run the information flow in business – Isolated islands, Interfaced bridges, and Integrated solutions.

Isolated islands are the most straightforward way most business owners manage a business manually. Paper is easily lost or rendered illegible, challenging to share with others without copying, and requires time to organize and file. Most will try to migrate to a computer by employing word processing files to keep notes. More adept users adopt spreadsheets for tracking everything from quotes, invoices, and bills. Over time, the owner has accumulated documents and spreadsheets lists for nearly every information need in the business, fulfilling Maslow's law of the instrument, "if all you have is a hammer, everything looks like a nail."[11]

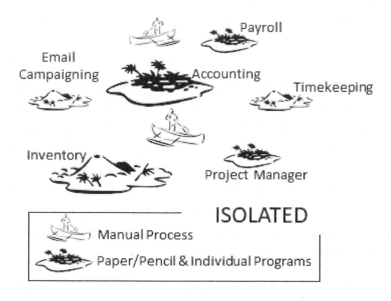

Even if one computerizes most manual processes, many other deficiencies will arise, from meaningful reports to data security. The labor cost involved in entering, updating, moving, and correcting data among the isolated islands is disproportionate to the desired outcome, profit.

The second means to manage data involves spending some *real* cash on an accounting system plus a subscription to an online marketing tool, like Constant Contact or Mailchimp. Before too long, the business has a rich toolset. "Toolset," you ask? Yes, toolset. Marketing prefers using Constant Contact while HR is using Mailchimp. The sales department has a Customer Relationship Manager (CRM), while purchasing is using just the accounts payable

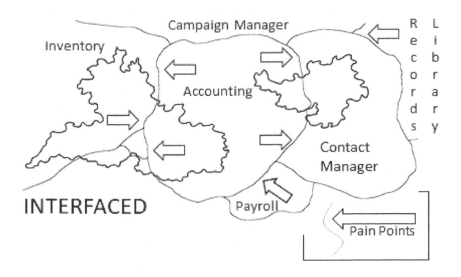

INTERFACED

and inventory modules in the accounting software, supplemented with spreadsheets.

Most owners will choose whatever software they or their reliable associates find accessible, cheaper, and available on the market. When transferring data from one application to another, increased labor costs add to these continual processes. **Interfacing** between 2 or more sets of information creates *pressure* or *pain points* where they are bridged. Imagine the San Andreas Fault, where two massive plates interface to form a fault. As these plates shift, the pressure builds, and earthquakes result, damaging the bridge and interrupting movement from one side to the other.

The same is true for interfaced computer programs. Routinely exporting your customer list from an accounting system to import it into an email management system each month will result in on-going labor costs. These will skyrocket if either system – accounting or email – has software changes. How often does that happen? Daily, as evidenced by significant updates downloaded onto millions of computers each week.

The third approach involves **integrating** various software programs. Most owners and entrepreneurs resist integration projects for a variety of reasons.[12] They fear they will never realize a reasonable rate of return. Owner uncertainty and doubt detected by employees fuels their resistance to embrace change and leads to a business-wide failure to support the project.[13]

Nevertheless, senior management must align the employees with the goals and objectives of the business. We know from experience that change is ever-present, and the WEF notes that to learn, unlearn, and relearn rapidly enough to keep pace with the increasing knowledge velocity are essential skills in the 4th Industrial Revolution.[3]

INTEGRATED

Building such a flexible team around integrated systems leads to repeated cost-savings.[12] For example, to store all business records in an electronic vault by simply dragging the file into a window and then retrieving it using a mere search-engine program can save the company $20/activity when compared to the manual filing.[15] McCorry further notes that it costs an average of $120 to find a single "lost" file and as much as $220 to rebuild an entire folder of records gone missing.[14]

Zety's editor, Bart Turczynski, reported that 250 candidates apply for each job listed.[16] Given 10 minutes to review a printed resume, the average time spent to find candidates can take more than 30 hours. Tasks include creating the job description, posting on job boards and other advertising venues, receiving and reviewing 250 resumes, and selecting three to six qualified candidates to interview for one position. Turczynski also noted that about 80% of all resumes contain intentional and unintentional wrong information.

Integrated workforce recruitment solutions for finding candidates exist that capture, validate, and reduce the identification time by more than 99%, but it calls for planning and investing time at the outset.[12] The potential gains are enormous as the business enters growth and scaling phases. To discuss the full impact of selecting the wrong candidate is beyond this chapter. Still, you can imagine costs mount higher, as do the distractions that accompany the wrong hire.[17] In this case, we recommend that small businesses hire slow and fire fast.[18]

Integrated Systems Restore Time

Today, as never before, affordable solutions exist that provide an integrated infrastructure for businesses based on more than the usual core accounting, inventory, and time-tracking programs. There are three major processes that, if addressed in an integrated manner, will lead to immediate and repetitive long-term time- and money-savings, while also eliminating pain points and future disruptions to the business. As already described, these include applicant recruitment-to-employee management, timekeeping to billing and payroll, and document management integrated with contact relationships involving vendors, employees, in addition to prospects and customers.

There are many challenges posed daily in every small and mid-size business across the country, and it's not too late to recognize the asset value of data within your company. Here are a few to consider in addition to the electronic filing and recruitment processes:

1. effectively emailing tailored communications to customers on a scale larger than one at a time;

2. rapidly pivoting and improving customer service and product delivery;

3. accurately processing customer orders;

4. creatively and efficiently prospecting for new leads;

5. finding and negotiating with strategic, dependable suppliers; and

6. proactively managing human capital after onboarding, from skill assessment and development to employee inclusion, as well as performance measures, and even proper termination.

Each of these activities consumes large amounts of time because they are necessary and repetitive. Integrated systems automatically share data across your business where needed, restoring minutes, hours, days, and even weeks to your timebank. The financial gains are also repetitive, like the manual processes that integration replaces. A dollar saved, over and over again. Besides, who wouldn't like more time to work on crucial, customer-facing, profit-generating activities every day?

Integrate for Well-Managed, Intentional Growth
Glossary:

Business-to-Business (B2B): Describes a specific relationship among two or more businesses, usually involving a commercial transaction, such as a customer sales order, a vendor purchase order, or a marketing campaign.

Business-to-Consumer (B2C): Describes a specific relationship between a business and consumers of its products or services, such as direct sales to individuals or families.

Big-Box Store: A description applied to a physically large retail store selling products in high-volume at lower market prices than smaller stores.

Contact or Customer Relationship Management (CRM): A technology for managing all business relationships and interactions, including customers and potential customers, and applicants, employees, contractors, and suppliers.

Disruption: A break or interruption in the ordinary course or continuation of some activity or process.

Fourth Industrial Revolution: The ongoing automation of traditional manufacturing and industrial practices, using modern smart technology.

General Data Protection Regulation (GDPR): A legal framework setting guidelines for the collection and processing of personal information from individuals who live in the European Union (EU).

Isolated Island (of Information): A computer-based system whose functions are independent of any other system, i.e. not related directly, information is disconnected from business processes, and data are neither shared nor exchanged with any other application.

Interfaced Bridge (for Information): A link between two computer-based systems that share or exchange data with each other on a limited basis, discretely exporting from one system in one step and importing into another as a second step. Information is connected to business processes, which can be interrupted when the link fails to operate.

Integrated Solution (or Integrated Systems of Information): A network among one or more computer-based systems that share or exchange data with each other as information is generated, continuously exporting from one system in one step and importing into another as a second step. Information is connected to business processes, but permit uninterrupted, independent operation of systems in the event a network fails.

Maslow's Law of the Instrument (or Maslow's hammer): A cognitive bias that involves an over-reliance on a familiar tool, dismissing any alternatives.

North American Industry Classification System (NAICS): A classification of business establishments by type of economic activity (a process of production) used by government and business in Canada, Mexico, and the United States of America.

Paradigm Shift: A significant change that occurs when a new and different way replaces common or traditional thinking about or doing something.

Workforce Recruitment and Development (Human Capital Management): The process of acquiring, training, managing, retaining employees for them to contribute effectively within the processes of the organization.

World Economic Forum (WEF): An international organization headquartered in Geneva, Switzerland, which brings together its membership annually to discuss major issues concerning the world political economy.

Meet Brilliant Practicing Expert™ Dennis Hill, Ph.D.:

Business-Technology Expert | Change Agent | C-Suite Leader Entrepreneur | Speaker | Educator

Self-described as *an engineer who can read financial statements,* Dr. Dennis Hill has been solving problems and making measurements in businesses for 40 years. He was introduced to computers at 14 and began his career as a research engineer with a major Fortune 100 company. Dr. Hill was the academic and administrative program head of one the first accredited undergraduate programs in computer science and engineering at 23, assisting other departments in developing additional degree programs in technical communication, business and computer science, and engineering management. His list of accomplishments, like his client list, are internationally recognized, pioneering many *firsts* in the fields of higher education, computer security, system performance, change management, and human resources.

As an innovator of technology solutions, Dennis has collaborated with scores of businesses over the years in manufacturing, distributing, retailing, hospitality, and entertainment to integrate and optimize their processes, people, and product lines for well-managed, intentional growth.

DENNIS' SPECIAL INVITATION FOR YOU: To learn more about integrating your business systems for well-managed, intentional growth, visit our resource center at:
https://www.IntegrateForGrowth.com and download our guide, "The Small Business Recipe – Integrating Ideas and Information".

⊠EXACTA

Business: EXACTA Corporation

EXACTA Corporation was established in 1976 early in the mainframe years of computing to assist banking, insurance, manufacturing, and other larger, enterprise-class companies. Our team of consultants has been industry pioneers in business computing, including blockchain, AI, and emerging 5G protocols.

To address small-to-medium business needs, EXACTA developed, sells, and supports CorporateOrganizer CRM&More, the first CRM to be built on data ownership and security laws while enabling companies to optimize and streamline company-wide information processes through a singular system that integrates with all others. Contact management for sales, workforce recruitment, and vendor management is built-in with tools for secure chatting within the company, document storing and searching, and extensions for time and billing, sales and marketing automation, and links to Quick-Books, Mailchimp, Constant Contact, and many other programs.

Website: htt ps://www.EXACTACorp.com

Connect with Dr. Hill and EXACTA on these social accounts:
LinkedIn: htt ps://www.LinkedIn.com/in/ManageChange
Twitter: htt ps://twitt er.com/EXACTACorp
Facebook: htt ps://www.facebook.com/exactacorp/

Download Mobile App: BrilliantBizBook from your App Store. It contains everything related to this Book Series and its Authors.

Allow Me to Introduce Brilliant Practicing Expert™

Melinda & Ryan Van Fleet, by Maggie Mongan

Do you ever get a great introduction that immediately makes sense? This is how I met Melinda Van Fleet – one part of a dynamic duo. I must admit I haven't spoken with Ryan nearly as much as Melinda because he's with customers for his charter business when we have most of our conversations. Ryan is a practical down to earth guy and is a go-getter. In fact, both the Van Fleets are extraordinary go-getters!

Both Melinda and Ryan had to reinvent themselves and their careers – all amidst a relocation halfway across the country. They failed, misstepped, and picked-up themselves, and one another, for daily rounds of improvements. Rebuilding, from the ground up isn't easy, it requires concentrated effort.

Small Business Owners consistently navigate challenging waters. When you have more confidence, you can be more productive and increase your revenue, while experiencing more peace. Individually, the Van Fleets speak and coach others on how to build their confidence and excel. Now they are teaming together and bringing their *confidence journey message* to the masses. Pay special attention to their practical approach to putting everything and everyone into their bucket system. Remember to take advantage of their offer at the bottom of their author's page to begin moving yourself in the right direction.

Building Confidence Along with a Successful Business – From the Ground Up

by Melinda & Ryan Van Fleet

I will never forget the day I looked at my husband Ryan and said, "You're getting your captain's license. You need to work for yourself." He stared at me. Probably scared sh$tless as we had no experience, business training, or money to start what is now *Good Karma Sportfishing.*

I remember when he got his captain's license, and we bought our boat, *The Good Karma.* The phone would ring with an inquiry, and he would look at me with a blank stare wondering what to say. We would scramble for words which eventually became a well-oiled script. Comments such as, "You must be a new captain" eventually subsided, and things got easier. What changed? Confidence.

I appreciate this quote by the Dalai Lama, "With realization in one's potential and self-confidence in one's ability, one can build a better world."[1]

Ryan started to build his confidence; hence, he's building a better world for himself and others.

What is Confidence?
Think about confidence for a second. What is your definition? How do you define it?

Do you get confused with *arrogance*? *Know it all*? Do you feel *proud*?

"Confidence is a belief in oneself, the conviction that one has the ability to meet life's challenges and to succeed—and the willingness to act accordingly. Being **confident** requires a realistic sense of one's capabilities and feeling secure in that knowledge."[2]

What are some words that come to mind regarding confidence?

Courage, fearless, risk-taker, balls, guts?

What are some negative words that come to mind regarding confidence?

Narcissist, arrogant, pompous?

Actor Stewart Stafford said, "Confidence is when you believe in yourself and your abilities, arrogance is when you think you are better than others and act accordingly."[3]

Balancing between confidence and arrogance can be tricky; however, knowing and understanding how you feel, or act is a key in being one or the other. Ryan and I often bounce thought processes off each other to ensure our actions are in the *positive bucket*.

TIP: Find someone you can talk to, if you aren't sure how your behaviors are being perceived.

Confidence is something we all need to appear more frequently in our business. Unfortunately, fear holds people back from building their confidence and sometimes even recognizing areas where they are confident.

There are many ways you can exhibit and build confidence:

- Business building and growth
- Communication

- Relationships
- Boundaries
- Personal health, wellness, and appearance

Similar to working out, building your confidence is like building muscles. It takes practice, hard work, and determination. All of us can do it.

When I interviewed John Lee Dumas (JLD), host of *Entrepreneurs on Fire* podcast, he said, "I think when it comes to confidence, a great thing to keep in mind is perspective. We are all not confident about certain things and number one, that's natural. That's normal. You're a human being."[4]

Confidence Regarding People, Relationships, and Communication

When I started as an Independent Sales Representative in 2009, I never lacked in confidence regarding cold calling, networking, and asking for the sale. I had the right balance and basic understanding after being a corporate buyer for 16 years. I felt confident in knowing how to build a relationship, add value, and have product knowledge. Where I quickly had to pick up some confidence was in dealing with people. Yes, dealing with customers was the hardest part.

Ryan and I quickly learned, not all people are nice. Some customers are demanding. Others may have high expectations, strange thought processes, or requests, etc. I am sure Ryan and I aren't alone.

I recall making my first sales trip. I conducted introduction phone calls to say "Hello" and mentioned I was going to be traveling to meet my new clients, face to face, and visit their store. The intention was a friendly sales visit to learn the territory. I remember how one account flipped out on me about coming to visit in offseason and she didn't want to place an order. By no means was I pressuring or even expecting an order — just a visit to introduce myself. Her behavior never improved.

I've run into a few accounts similar to her over the past ten years — they don't change. I have learned to conduct background research and have conversations with other sales reps in the same territory to see if their behavior is a trend. It usually is.

Instead of spending energy, time, and resources trying to manage the situation, it's simply best to walk away or give space. The more I practiced this, the more confident I became in trusting my gut when making choices. The great news is better customers appeared. I learned my time and energy is better spent helping them versus focusing on challenging customers.

Once I realized this was a win in my *confidence bucket*, we started applying it to *Good Karma Sportfishing*. Sure enough, the same results occurred. As Ryan's confidence grew in turning down charters for a multitude of reasons, better clients came along. The better clients appreciated his time, talent, fun attitude, and persistence on the water. They had a memorable and incredible trip. Building confidence was a win-win for everyone and has led to increased repeat business.

Confidence to Know When Something Doesn't Work for You or Sound Right to You

Ryan and I have taken risks, and not all of them have worked out. One example is when we had connected with a fishing lure maker, based in Mexico. We asked to be the US-based distributor of his product. We worked extremely hard for a year and a half on this business.

The business was about to turn a profit when the maker decided to compete against us with his website. His website was written in English, had a stronger URL than ours, and featured shipping anywhere in the world.

He thought his behavior was acceptable and we would continue to work with him. It was not acceptable, and we pulled out quickly. All three of those factors made him a competitor. We were confident in our decision and we were clear on what we brought to the table. It was the right decision.

As Professional Speaker and CEO of Holla Productions, Judi Holler shared during an interview on *The Good Karma Success Coach Podcast Episode 74*, "No Mistakes Only Gifts. It's this idea that you're either going to win or learn, but you will never lose. You only lose if you allow your mindset to take you to that place. When instead you choose to only seeing your life through the lens of possibility and positivity, you really become unstoppable."[5]

When you reframe your thinking of mistakes, the pressure is off. Everyone has *gifts*, but it's *how* you move through them and *apply* the learnings that ultimately drive you toward success. When we stopped working with the lure maker, we never thought of it as a mistake. *Gifts* came from the experience and we were grateful.

You may also experience a setback. A setback can propel you to pivot or tweak your business in new ways. Ryan and I often use setbacks as fuel. It's motivation to get through challenges and move forward in our business. Spending time wallowing in the mud doesn't help. Wallowing only creates negative forces, which ultimately slow you down.

A better word than setback is evolving. Many entrepreneurs evolve; unfortunately, not too many share this part of the journey.

Confidence to Forge Your Own Path

It's essential to have enough confidence to say "no" to an opportunity.

Ryan often receives opportunities to take others fishing on their boats. For years we regularly discussed this and shut the door quickly. The discussion dives into many variables, which would be part of or result in accepting the opportunity. Some of the things we consider are:

- Is the opportunity on-brand?
- How does it make him feel?
- Is it worth his time?
- Is there information he wishes to share in that format?
- What will the outcome be?

Real-world Confidence Story

When Covid-19 started, Ryan finally had time to start working on his courses. Offering courses to his audience for fishing tips, and ideas has been a discussion for a long time. I have purchased many courses on courses, read books, listened to podcasts, and every time I would bring up someone's course process i.e., funnels, challenges, webinars, lead magnets, affiliates, etc. Ryan wasn't interested.

We finally came up with the idea that works for him: sharing his mindset, time, ideas, and authentic nature. We decided to offer videos, varying in price, and let them be evergreen on our Shopify website. Whenever he has time, he creates a new course and promotes it to the level he feels is best. This process has proved very successful and built his confidence.

Not everything fits the brand. An owner selling a fishing product called asking to be featured on Ryan's Podcast, *Good Karma*

Sportfishing. He was looking to be a guest and talk about his product. Ryan only talks about the products he regularly uses and how they perform. We asked for the company to send us some products to try. They never did. The same company appeared on another podcast very quickly after our conversation. This made us believe that podcast probably hadn't tried the product and may have taken advantage of their audience.

NOTE: It's good to understand what boundaries you wish to set for your company and brand. Then develop a clear vision. Sticking with that vision and measuring the results will build your confidence toward future decisions.

Creating a Level of Confidence in Your Mind and Support Systems

Seeking wisdom from others can help build your confidence. You may have thoughts or ideas and doubt yourself. Perhaps you read something which triggered a formerly buried idea. The other person's mindset and content brought it back to life and fueled you with the courage and confidence to move forward.

To build confidence: surround yourself with support or create a mastermind like JLD mentions below and keep a positive forward movement perspective. "You always have to reground yourself. And that's why I'm a huge believer in being part of a mastermind. Surrounding yourself with people who you know, like, trust, and most importantly, really respect in your industry."[6]

It's easy to start your own mastermind or other groups. Don't be overwhelmed. It may take some time, but it's not difficult. I started a mastermind with two fellow speakers I met through a course last year. We *zoom* once a month and it has been extremely helpful in learning tips, keeping each other motivated, bouncing ideas, and networking. Consistently, make an effort to reach out and build your relationships.

On the flip side, recognize when you need to let go of some relationships or take a step back. When we first moved to The Keys, we met another couple who seemed supportive. As we grew our business, we could feel their energy shift. They started making odd comments, and the vibe changed. We had to walk away from this couple. It was okay to let them go. As you build your confidence, you will notice it's natural for some relationships to ebb and flow.

The 3 Action Steps to Create Unstoppable Confidence™

Unstoppable Confidence Step 1 - Identify:
Sit down, take a journal, a pad of paper, your phone, or whatever works for you, and write down the area(s) where you desire to build confidence.

Step 1 Bonus Tip: I talk about putting things into *buckets* while coaching and on my podcast *Crush It In Sales*. Putting skills, desires, or even people into buckets can help you prioritize, manage expectations, or edit these. It's an easy way to categorize and make something less daunting.

In regard to the areas where you need to build confidence, make a list by creating columns, and listing each trait under a *bucket* by the level of difficulty. Bucket 1 is the least difficult to Bucket 3 being the most difficult. Examples:

> Bucket 1: Need confidence in regularly executing social media posts.
>
> Bucket 2: Need confidence in executing social media posts when I am promoting my business.
>
> Bucket 3: Need confidence in doing live videos to promote my business.

Unstoppable Confidence Step 2 - Intention:

Think about "Your WHY"; per Simon Sinek.[7] Your WHY is fundamental in everything you do. The majority of people do not sit and think about their WHY. They may think about it briefly and then move on versus incorporating it into their lives, daily thought patterns, and choices. The choices you make will define you. If you circle back and remember your WHY as you make those choices, you will stay on the right path.

Step 2 Bonus Tip: Circle back on the things you're good at and areas you're already confident. Think about how you became confident in those areas.

What were the setbacks you used as fuel to keep going? What was your WHY when you were going through a challenge? Is there something you achieved and had forgotten about?

Take time to reflect. Often, we're so busy going through our life and our daily routine that we don't reflect enough to set ourselves up for success.

Unstoppable Confidence Step 3 - Action:

What actions are you going to take? Depending on what it is, it could be small steps – daily, weekly, or monthly. When we were taking action steps toward building a community, it seemed scary and daunting. As time went by with each step, it became easier and more fun.

Step 3 Bonus Tip: When you make a plan and think about your WHY, it creates motivation and reason. We all need motivation and reason. Without it, there is no reason to do anything. You are hungry, so you eat. You are tired, so you sleep. Understanding the motivation behind your plan is as simple as breaking it down into basic reasons.

When you use the breakdown approach, it's not so scary. Once you realize the things you've done before that got you where you are today, it becomes obvious and achievable.

Each of us has infinite potential to be successful. Some of these steps may seem simple but aren't always easy. It's the consistent work, over time, that creates the results. Most people don't do the work and this is why they don't succeed. Time goes by quickly. Create daily, weekly, or monthly steps to increase your confidence.

Ryan and I continue to fine-tune our confidence on a daily basis. We follow the steps above and pivot along the way. Things do have a way of working themselves out and we learn from any *gifts*. Those *gifts* make us stronger so we can consistently elevate our business and help others along the way too.

REMEMBER:
The powerful combination of believing in yourself and taking action creates confidence, and you will be unstoppable.

Building Confidence Along with
a Successful Business – From the Ground Up
Glossary:

Cold Calling: Process of reaching out to a potential client/customer that you do not know and starting a relationship that could result in business.

Confidence: A feeling of self-assurance arising from one's appreciation of one's own abilities or qualities.

Confidence Bucket: A systematic way of grouping categories together to help take action and minimize any anxiety.

Courage: Strength in the face of a difficult or challenging situation.

Fearless: Ability to take action and not be afraid of the outcome.

Mastermind: An organized group of like-minded individuals who regularly meet to discuss and strategize ideas.

Mindset: A well-established set of beliefs held by an individual that guides actions.

Motivation: Desire to act or behave in a certain way.

Positive Bucket: A way to categorize good actions that have happened or are predicted to happen.

Reason: Thought process around why a decision was made.

Repeat Business: Client/customer who chooses to do business again.

Risk Taker: A person who is willing to do or try things in order to achieve a goal.

Setback: A temporary stall or reversal of an action.

Support Systems: A person or group of people that provide advice, feedback, ideas in a positive way.

Unstoppable: Not able to hold back.

Your WHY: An understanding of what drives you to take action.

Zoom: A video and web conferencing platform used to communicate.

Meet Brilliant Practicing Experts™ Melinda & Ryan Van Fleet:

Success Coaches | Professional Speakers | Small Business Owners and an Obsessed Sportfishing Captain

Melinda and Ryan Van Fleet lost their corporate jobs at the same time in 2009. Instead of focusing on their setback, they packed their belongings and headed to The Florida Keys to begin the second act they had envisioned.

Ryan Van Fleet built his successful fishing charter business *Good Karma Sportfishing*, podcast *Good Karma Sportfishing Podcast,* and thriving community, based on the values of persistence, confidence, collaboration, having fun, and catching big fish!

Melinda Van Fleet is a multi-passionate success coach who built her coaching, speaking, and writing on the values of helping others believe in themselves and take action. Melinda believes many women are stuck and unfulfilled their potential.

Together they make a powerful team helping empower individuals and couples to live their best lives. They strongly believe that if they can do it, you can do it too.

MELINDA & RYAN'S SPECIAL INVITATION FOR YOU:

Sign up for a free video training to discover how you can build or level up your confidence and maximize your potential. Go to:
https://goodkarmaconfidence.com

Businesses: Good Karma Success Coach & Good Karma Sportfishing

When the Van Fleets started over from scratch, Melinda always said, "Someday we will help others." Even when things were tough, and they didn't know if they could pay rent, they kept going. They always kept the vision and goal in mind.

After building their core businesses for 9 years, they formed The Good Karma Success Coach. Their intention was to take all the valuable business and life lessons compiled over 25 years of experience and create an inspirational business that can impact lives.

The Van Fleets Signature *Unstoppable Confidence Course* and *The 3 Action Steps to Create Unstoppable Confidence*™ help clients get unstuck and move towards action. As a result, clients take powerful action in which they can transform to live their potential in business, relationships, and life in general.

Websites: https://goodkarmasuccesscoach.com
https://goodkarmasportfishing.com

Connect with Ryan on these social accounts:
LinkedIn: https://linkedin.com/in/ryan-van-fleet-goodkarma
Facebook: https://facebook.com/Capt.RyanGoodKarmaSportfishing
Instagram: @goodkarmasportfishing_fl_keys
Mobile App: Good Karma Sportfishing

Connect with Melinda on these social accounts:
LinkedIn: https://linkedin.com/in/melinda-van-fleet/
Instagram: @melinda_vanfleet
Facebook: https://facebook.com/melinda.vanfleet.315

Download Mobile App: BrilliantBizBook from your App Store.
It contains everything related to this Book Series and its Authors.

PERFORMANCE
PILLAR 4

PEACEFULNESS

Allow Me to Introduce Brilliant Practicing Expert™

Dr. Jyun Shimizu, by Maggie Mongan

When I first met Dr. Jyun, I was astonished by his high level of energy and optimism. Admittedly, I should have expected this after I heard how he was an exceptional person and excelled at his expertise.

When we converse, Dr. Jyun is very attentive – a rare find these days when we are speaking with health/wellness professionals. His perspective is not new; yet, our science has finally evolved to validate these ancient teachings and practices. As more people have become disenchanted with modern techniques and practices, Dr. Jyun's perspective is welcomed as a fresh and simplistic approach to wellness and performance.

Since the inception of this book series, I have sought to find an expert who would address, (a) you, Small Busines Owner, as the greatest asset of your business, (b) share applicable wisdom to assist you in succeeding, and (c) provide science, strategies, and tactics you could apply to improve your business's performance, as well as your own performance.

During 2020, many Small Business Owners where challenged and / or thrusted to release some of their ineffective beliefs and approaches. Solution? Dr. Jyun. He is equipped with science, simplified wisdom, and proven practices to advance your mission. Remember to take advantage of his next steps at the bottom of his author's page.

Uncover Your Cells' Stories, Discover Your Quantum Nature™
You are the Best Asset of Your Business

by Jyun Shimizu, I-MD, Ph.D.

Dear Small Business Owners,

The following is the key to the creation of abundance in a small business, both financially and relationally.

Health, by definition, is the condition when the mind, body, and spirit are in balance. To experience the continuation of feeling "well," we must pay attention to all three areas and keep the physical, mental, and spiritual part of yourself in harmony.

Question: do you think personal well-being has anything to do with the health of your business? How you show up in business is a direct reflection of who you are. You are the greatest asset to your business.

Founder of business energetic and author of *Undoubtedly Awesome*, Anne Tucker shares, "It's all your energy. Your energy is the blueprint for whatever you're casting out into the world."[1] You must start within your health and well-being by paying attention to yourself physically, mentally, and spiritually.

Abundance in Business and Personal Life

Business is about the creation and expression of your ultimate fulfillment from your heart. Without joy in your heart, anything you do becomes meaningless. Co-founder of ISAMIZU, Dr. Isabel Perez, states, "The core values of your business should be in sync with your values, and with the desire of your heart and soul."[2]

Human beings, including you, are here to expand and elevate our consciousness through our *genius*. Real financial success and abundance will always follow when your *purpose* comes in alignment with the non-ego centered self. Let us open the door and allow me to invite you to discover and unlock Your Quantum Nature™ to transform you into the best version of yourself on both your business and personal level. You will achieve your *flow state* and meaningful life.

Which Lens (Perspective) Do You Wear to See the World?

As a small business owner or entrepreneur, you have or will experience uncertainty, self-doubt, worries, and perhaps anxiety. Presently, in the year 2020, we are experiencing unprecedented events; critical economic, social, and political shifts are inevitable in the coming years.

I would like you, as a small business owner, to take a moment and contemplate the following question:

What is the difference between the person who expands and thrives in the business world versus the person who contracts and languishes when undergoing significant stress? Aside from situational differences that are usually out of an individual's control, the only difference is perspective.

All of us choose a particular mind lens to view the external world. Do you see conflicts or challenges as opportunities of abundance or scarcity? In other words, do you see a glass half full or a glass half empty?

When you have a different perspective in a challenging situation, it produces different feelings. One makes you positive and excited, and perhaps others make you worried or concerned. Preferably, you would like to wear the lens that makes you empowered, motivated, and energized, right?

JYUN SHIMIZU, I-MD, PH.D.

Realization of Your Specific Lens (Perspective

By the age of 7 years old, you have already developed specific blueprints in your unconscious mind through your external environments like parents, grandparents, and siblings. With this blueprint (perspective and belief, you start seeing and experiencing the human world combined with your inherited imprints from your ancestry. Therefore, your thoughts are limited and repeated regularly through unconscious belief.

Most of us experience unwanted negative emotions, habits, and behaviors from the above external environment. No wonder we deal with many mental and psychological challenges in daily life as an adult. Unconsciously, we often feel pessimistic and have a negative attitude towards life and business when faced with a stressful situation.

How to Wear Your New Lens (New Perspective

According to the new genetic study called Epigenetics, external and internal environments can influence the genetic representation and manifest the person you are now. To have desirable physical and mental health, you must immerse yourself in a different external environment than currently surrounds you. Moreover, you, yourself, illuminate as a positive person and carry abundance within.

There is a famous concept called *The Law of Attraction.* When you are positive and optimistic, you often find yourself surrounded by positive people. Dr. Isabel, Co-founder of ISAMIZU, also said, "Our thoughts affect our emotions. If our thoughts are positive, our emotions will reflect the same. The evolution of the business, as well as your personal life, will be successful with a positive mindset."[2]

A Perfect Storm in Health and Business

Two hundred fifty million adults are living in the United States. One-third of American adults (approximately 83 million) are experiencing nervousness, anxiety, fatigue, or irritability due to stress. About 50 percent of American adults (125 million) have difficulties sleeping due to stress.[3]

Chronic stress can result in severe health conditions, including anxiety, insomnia, muscle pain, high blood pressure, and a weakened immune system.[4] About 100 million adults in the United States were affected by chronic pain, including joint pain or arthritis.[5]

Chronic pain is an additional epidemic and has become a significant concern for small business owners and their health. Among chronic illnesses, the three significant illnesses affecting American adults are heart disease, cancer, and diabetes. The annual social and economic cost of those three significant diseases had reached over 1 trillion dollars in 2010.[6]

Let's look at the following facts. In the US, over 99 percent of America's 28.7 million firms are small businesses. The vast majority (88 percent of employer firms have fewer than 20 employees, and nearly 40 percent of all enterprises have under $100k in revenue.[7] Small businesses are the anchor of the US economy.

What does this all mean? At least 10 million small business owners are overly stressed and have significant health issues. How can small business owners produce financial and relational health in business while they are suffering from chronic stress and illness? Despite increasing business revenue and significant economic growth in the US year after year, people are more stressed and spending more money on substantial health issues than ever before.

Question: Is this a desirable future for the upcoming generation? If you answered NO to this question, I encourage you to discover the solution and shift towards personal and business health growth.

Discovery of Mind-Body Connection

We often search for solutions that reside outside ourselves. What I am going to say is this: the answer lies within yourself. I would like to propose to you the process that could change the way you view your overall health as well as the financial and relational health of your small business.

There is a leading-edge study in Neuroscience called PsychoNeuroEndoImmunology (PNEI. It means that your mind (Psycho affects your brain (Neuro, your brain (Neuro affects your hormonal system (Endo, and your hormones affect your immune system (Immune. Your thoughts can influence your physical health and well-being.

Neuroscientific research explains how a thought produces a specific feeling and emotion, and the brain generates a specific neuropeptide in response to this feeling and emotion. The brain sends this signal, in the form of a neuropeptide, to a particular receptor in the body, which tells your cells how to act—whether in a healthy and balanced manner or in a protective manner that may create negative stress on the body.

The Mindset Pattern Trap

For instance, when your mind decides to create a feeling of fear, your brain sends neuro signals to the kidneys. In this case, your kidneys receive excessive fear signals and it can create an imbalance with the heart. Interestingly enough, your heart reflects the feeling of love and also resides next to one of the most powerful immune systems called the thymus gland. The over-dominant emotion of fear will weaken the energy of the heart and function of the thymus gland. Dr. Carla Burns, I-MD, Ph.D., stated, "If your mind and your thoughts are not in alignment with your heart, that is going to create disease and stress."[8]

People are very fearful of uncertain economic forecasts, never-ending COVID-19 pandemic changes, and an unpredictable climate and what this means for the future of small business. Most people perceive recent major events fearfully, thereby inhibiting the process of their own immune function.

Prolonged chronic stress promotes secondary diseases such as depression, heart disease, allergies, women's hormonal issues, and insomnia. Having emotional, psychological, and physical health problems won't help the performance of your small business growth and expansion. What are the solutions for this trapped pattern?

Your Quantum Nature™ Formula

To manifest your best as a small business entrepreneur, YOU need to be the best. Expression of *Your Quantum Nature*™ (YQN™ with purpose and intention will lead you to abundance in your personal life and your small business entrepreneurship. Let's dive into this Triangle success formula, untrain what you know, and retrain, in a conscious way, to upgrade yourself. There are THREE facets to this formula to become the best version of yourself: One is the Quantum body, the second is the Quantum mind, and the third is the soul/spirit.

YQN ™ is the dynamic balance between the Quantum body and the Quantum mind. It is the ultimate feedback loop that results in the expression of who you are. The Quantum body and the Quantum mind are in constant co-creation of who you are, and we can experience ultimate bliss and reach our greatest potential when the body, mind, and spirit are in alignment.

You can have the ultimate mindset, but if you ignore the importance of your physical body, your mind won't work efficiently. Conversely, you can focus solely on being in better shape physically through daily exercise, eating well, and good sleep; yet, if your mind creates negative emotions, it is difficult for the physical body to be in sync with your mind. Without a sense of clear soul purpose, your creation and fulfillment won't be sustainable.

Allow me to explain further.

There are five human essentials, *The Five Conscious ISAMIZU Actions*™, to shift from a passive state into a proactive state. The mastery of these actions will help rebuild a healthy physical and mental balance, "your powerful engine," to support the production of abundance in business. Please remind yourself, your approach towards health and wellness will reflect the way you manage and operate your small business.

The First Step Towards the Best Version of Yourself

The Five ISAMIZU Conscious Actions™

Action 1: Conscious Breathing

Did you know this one simple technique can change your stress response as well as reverse many chronic diseases? Many scientific studies have researched the importance of breathing, such as Relaxation Response by Dr. Hebert Benson, TM meditation, Heart Rate Variability (HRV) breathing, and many more.

The parasympathetic nervous system is designed to calm your stress response, provide balance, and support your physical organs and cells. One of the best ways to activate your parasympathetic nervous system is to practice deep breathing. When you quiet your mind and observe the subtleties of breathing, you will not only gain an awareness of your internal state, but also stimulate your vagus nerve which helps control the relaxation response of the heart, lungs, and digestive tract. When our bodies are in their most relaxed state, healing occurs. We heal ourselves when we are most at ease and our creative energy is most abundant.

TIP: 15 minutes of daily conscious breathing practice will help restore the autonomic nervous system balance and improve coherence between the heart and the mind.

Action 2: Conscious Water Intake

Do you know how much water is required for your body to function correctly? According to many types of research, a healthy body needs a quarter to half the body weight in ounces of clean water. Water is a semi-conductor of electricity and has the vital ability to hold memory. Every single cell has to communicate with each other through water (more specifically, electrons between atoms, H_2O). Memory is stored in water based on the frequency, vibration, and energy of each word, sound, color, thought, emotion, and any other environmental energetic influences.

Michiko Hayashi, Ambassador and Global Director of non-profit organization Emoto Peace Project, said, "Water has a memory. Based on your particular emotion, your water structure expresses differently. When we create positive emotions, words, or thoughts, the water molecule shows a beautiful harmonic crystal. On the other hand, negative emotions, words, or thoughts express disturbing and disorganized crystal structure."[9]

The average adult's cell contains 65% water. We have about 100 trillion cells in our body. It is evident how having positive thoughts, emotions, and words is indispensable to create a healthy body and a healthy business. Michiko Hayashi continues, "For anyone who's starting a business, try to have positive people around you because everybody or everything is energy and your energy affects other people. People around you have their energy, and if they are positive, their positive energy will help you also."[9]

TIP: Before you drink a glass of water, hold the glass in both hands, and create a positive thought for your water—love, compassion, gratitude.

Action 3: Conscious Nutrition

You've probably heard the old saying, "You are what you eat." Nutrition is the fuel for your engine to generate your mental and physical power. Have you seen a two-stroke lawnmower that requires an oil/gas mixed fuel in their tank? If you combine the wrong ratio of oil and gas, your engine won't work effectively. It is the same with your cells. The mitochondria in your cells function as your body's engine and require specific fuel to function.

As unique individuals, we have different DNA expressions based on our ancestry. Your motor, the mitochondrial engine, is unique and specific to your cells. It requires a particular ratio of fats and carbohydrates to generate optimum vitality. Imagine being full of energy and having mental clarity all day. You can gracefully overcome your challenges and immensely increase your productivity through conscious nutrition.

TIP: Always eat organic, natural, and fresh produce according to your DNA/Blood Type and Dosha Type. The most critical recommendation is to "chew" food REALLY well (30x per mouthful in your mouth until there are no longer any textures before swallowing.

Quantum Creation of Your Financial Abundance

As you learn the importance of the first three conscious actions, you begin to understand the complexity and continuous evolution of your Quantum mind, body, and spirit. By adding the other 2 conscious actions, which you will find at the bottom of my Author Page at the end of this chapter, you will experience the clear awareness of mind-body conscious connection. If put into practice, it will enrich your life experience and bring the unshakable foundation to build your success.

Remember: everything is energy, especially us. When you are at the highest level of vibration and potential energy, your small business will have a high level of peak performance. You will achieve any success in your small business by unleashing your full potential by *embodying Your Quantum Nature*™.

Your financial abundance and fulfillment are right here, right now.

Uncover Your Cells' Stories, Discover Your Quantum Nature™ You are the Best Asset of Your Business
Glossary:

Blueprint: A framework that you acquire in your unconscious mind.

Consciousness: Awareness of your surroundings.

Your Quantum Nature™ (YQN™): Each of us has a unique expression based on genealogical information stored in our DNA and selection of specific DNA signal expression. The different combinations of our genes with the particular signal expression is what makes us unique. The underlying emotional, psychological, and external environmental factors affect the subtle systems within our body that alter our energetic imprint and cause disorder, unbalance, and disease.

Your quantum nature™ has into consideration ALL the characteristics that influence and are part of our essence in complete Homeostasis, health, and well-being. To be in Your Quantum Nature, there are multiple aspects to be considered to achieve balance, including and not limited to genetics, epigenetics, emotions, and psychology.

Flow State: Be in a zone of an altered state of consciousness. You feel bliss, joy, and happiness when you perform a task with little efforts.

PNEI (Psychoneuroendoimmunology): The study of the interaction between psychological processes and the nervous and immune systems of the human body.

Quantum Body: Dynamic nature of the body that interact with mind and consciousness.

Quantum Mind: Dynamic nature of the mind that interact with body and consciousness.

Coherence: The state of unity and work as a whole.

Relaxation Response by Dr. Hebert Benson: The ability to encourage your body to release chemicals and brain signals that make your muscles and organs slow down and increase blood flow to the brain.

TM meditation: A silent mantra meditation led by Mararishi Mahesh Yogi.

HRV (Heart Rate Variability): There are a natural physiological phenomenon that occurs between heartbeats as a variation of time intervals.

Autonomic Nervous System (ANS): Contains two divisions the sympathetic nervous system and the parasympathetic nervous system. These two nervous systems regulate bodily functions.

Parasympathetic Nervous System: The nervous system in charge of rest and digestion.

Vagus Nerve: The tenth cranial nerve in charge of communication between the digestive system and the organs to the brain and vice versa.

Two-stroke lawn mower: The engine has a single fill port for both the engine oil and gas. Without proper proportions between gas and oil, the engine won't work properly.

Mitochondria: An organelle found in most cells. It generates the energy called ATP that will lead to your vitality.

Epigenetics: The study of changes in organisms occurred by modification of gene expression, not an alternation of the genetic code itself.

Blood Type Diet: A type of eating that based on an individual blood type.

DNA Diet: According to nutrigenomics, the person's nutritional need will be analyzed by the genetic makeup and information through DNA testing.

Dosha Type Diet (The ayurvedic diet): A type of eating plan that arrange guideline for when, how, and what you should eat based on your Dosha or Body type.

Meet Brilliant Practicing Expert™ Jyun Shimizu, I-MD, Ph.D.:

Doctor of Integrative Medicine I Quantum Health Consultant #1 Bestselling Author I Speaker Conscious Wellness Expert

Dr. Jyun was inspired by his family's value of compassion, a balanced diet, and natural healing in Japan. The last 25 years of his medical and healing expertise led him to earn his doctorate and Ph.D. in integrative medicine with Quantum Principle. With his true holistic and integrative approach towards healing, he is clearly able to identify everyone's needs to liberate from suffering and help empower people to take control of their health and well-being. He is a person of passion with enthusiastic energy. It is contagious to be around him. He is an active author, publicly speaks to help others seek their own truth, and consults around the world.

DR. JYUN'S SPECIAL INVITATION FOR YOU:

Learn more about how to complete *The Five Conscious Actions*™ to build your health and wellness foundation and receive the free video to start your journey. **Go to: https://ISAMIZU.com/education**

Business: ISAMIZU, LLC

Dr. Jyun is a co-founder of ISAMIZU, LLC, which is a Global Conscious Wellness Organization with a worldwide teaching learning community, as well as a company that creates empowering resources to promote health and wellness with consciousness.

Dr. Isabel (co-founder and Dr. Jyun provide pathways through the latest breakthroughs of modern science and ancient science with technology to empower you to take control of your health and well-being. Together, they build the community to support each other for the future generation.

As a team of Quantum Health Consultants, combined over 45 years of various experiences in medicine and healing, they will uncover your, your family's, or your team's sufferings and challenges. They will discover *Your Quantum Nature*™ to achieve the highest potentials in your business and personal success.

Websites: https://ISAMIZU.com https://DRJYUN.com

Connect with Dr. Jyun and ISAMIZU on these social accounts:
LinkedIn: https://www.linkedin.com/in/drjyun
https://www.linkedin.com/in/isamizu-global
Instagram: @isamizu.global, @Dr.Jyun
Facebook: https://www.facebook.com/ISAMIZU.GLOBAL
YouTube: http://youtube.com/c/ISAMIZUGLOBAL
Author Profile: https://www.amazon.com/author/drjyun

Download Mobile App: BrilliantBizBook from your App Store.
It contains everything related to this Book Series and its Authors.

Allow Me to Introduce Brilliant Practicing Expert™

Maggie Mongan, by Lori Bonaparte of TrueYouInAction.com

I can summarize Maggie Mongan in three words: She consistently over-delivers!

I met Maggie at a business conference in 2012. We soon developed a habit of frequent calls. This led to an exchange of business ideas and a deep personal friendship, which we refer to as our, "World Domination Partnership!" We've challenged each other to stretch into the best versions of ourselves, cheered each other on, and helped the other to pivot and regroup as necessary.

I've come to appreciate her business acumen, emotional intelligence, intuition, and wisdom. I have gleaned much from her innovative business strategies, as well as her vast knowledge of human behavior and relational skills. All of which, she shares so generously.

Years ago, the book you're holding began as one of Maggie's *simple ideas*. Efficiently assembling business strategies from various experts – she didn't stop there. Since then, she has grown it into an annual book series, complete with its own mobile app, podcast, and virtual summit!

Do you see a pattern? Whatever you come to expect from Maggie, she will find ways to surprise you by delivering more.

In life, there are those who meet minimum expectations on the value they deliver, and then there are those who occasionally deliver a little extra. Then, there's Maggie, who consistently over-delivers!

How Valuing Your Values
Adds Value to Your Business

by Rev. Maggie Mongan, CEO

Are you one of the Small Business Owners who is always being pulled in many different directions? This appears to be an epidemic in small businesses. How many times have you already had this happen today? The good news and bad news are the same: you are not alone!

For almost the past 20 years, I've been guiding small business owners and business leaders to optimize their business performance and leadership. During this time, many challenges haven't changed, except adding social media and automation to our demanding activities. What is the primary challenge of business ownership? Determining which activities and/or projects are truly priorities.

It may be disappointing to learn this answer isn't found in business textbooks. Many experts are priceless when you need to deep dive into a particular aspect of your business; yet, most experts won't discuss this topic because they typically look through the myopic lens of their expertise. It's untouchable by many experts, even productivity experts because it goes beyond the *Science of Business*—the nuts and bolts of business, which is factual and undeniable. Today, we will discuss the *Art of Business* and you will be able to increase your peace and profitability as you begin *The Small Business Core Values Initial Inquiry*™.

What Adds Value to Your Business?

Surprisingly, one of the things which adds significant value to your business has nothing to do with finances; however, it will increase your profitability and business's valuation. Values, and core values, have been overlooked by business experts for decades. This subtle topic, when mastered, has a profound impact on businesses.

In an article Jim C. Collins wrote, he shares how some of the most successful businesses—Disney, Hewlett-Packard (HP), and Boeing— have positioned their business' core values as essential and used values to guide their growth and sustainability. In fact, when Collins was referencing how to effectively navigate through change, he reveals, "Change is good—but first know what should never change."[1] Collins was referencing using a business's values as the steady anchor through any storm.

What are Values and Core Values?

According to BusinessDictionary.com, core values are defined as: "Important and lasting beliefs or ideals shared by the members of a culture . . . about what is good or bad and desirable or undesirable. Values have a major influence on a person's behavior and attitude and serve as broad guidelines in all situations."[2]

Let's simplify this definition. Why? One of my core values is *simplicity*, so I'm constantly helping SBOs simplify things for practical and applicable purposes.

Think of values as what is most important to you. Values are your beliefs, attitudes, and behaviors. These beliefs are called values because you treasure them. Your personal values may be similar or completely different from your business's values.

CLUE: Some people talk about how our attitudes and behaviors are *expressions* of our beliefs or values.

Stephen R. Covey stated, "Peace of mind comes when your life is in harmony with true principles and values".[3] Assume the same is true for your business.

Are you experiencing resistance, overwhelm, or frustration? Your beliefs, actions, or attitudes may be misaligned with your deep truths or values. Jon Stewart shared, "If you don't stick to your values where they're being tested, they're not values: they're hobbies."[4]

Core Values are Your Business's Anchor to Treasures

Anchors keep vessels from drifting. Core values is another concept often mentioned when people are having conversations about values. Do you ever find yourself disregarding what you promised? What about promises which pull you in different directions? Values keep you from drifting away from your goals and commitments.

Typically, core values are considered your most significant three key values. These three values tend to be your steady anchors throughout any experience. Stephane & Shalee Schafeitel teach, "There's power in identifying your three core values."[5] Three core values provide us a simple check-in list to assure our actions and attitude align with our authentic self.

Core values are intrinsic. They are your foundational values. "Your core values are much more than your typical values – this set of values goes much deeper. These values are unwavering and always guide you. You may be honoring them without any conscious thoughts. Core values run deep within your mental programming to guide your thoughts, actions,"[6] and attitudes.

INSIGHT: Throughout life's experiences, you've been assigning values to what you've observed. Over time, this creates certain aspects of your personality and how you choose to show up.

Example: "If you had an experience which impacted you about tenderness or someone honoring something and it deeply touched you, reverence may be one of your core values. These words have unspoken depth – they speak to you at your core."[7]

Oversimplified, think of values as part of the way you express what you highly appreciate. "The core values of an organization are those values we hold at the foundation of which we perform work and conduct ourselves."[8] As time changes focus, projects, and priorities change, "values underlie our work, how [we] interact with each other, and which strategies we employ to fulfill our mission."[9]

WARNING: Goals are not values, strategies, what you stand for, nor opinions. You may have a goal to financially survive through a difficult stormy phase—like the global pandemic of 2020, or The Great Recession of 2008; however, this goal isn't a value. Values "allow us to persevere through adversity."[10]

Values are Your Unidentified Driver

Values are what help you accomplish your goals. They are constantly guiding you on how to show up—with integrity to yourself, your business, and your loved ones.

Once you begin identifying your values, you will notice how your business's success is either amplified by the alignment of activities and values or it is devastated by the misalignment. Further, the same is true for your performance. Isn't it odd how your values show up, revealing who you are? What's even more remarkable is how your values are more noticeable to others than to you.

One of the resistant points some Small Business Owners (SBOs) have to success is factual—some successful people sell out. My clients have said, "I'd rather sabotage myself because I don't want to compromise my integrity." I get it! What if you don't have to sell out?

What if you're already selling out on your values in ways you haven't considered? Any broken promises? "Honoring our word, not just a spoken word, means the alignment of our attitudes, decisions, behaviors, and actions are aligned with our values and in alignment with our vision."[11] The same holds true for your business's vision.

You, SBO, are the leader of your business. Kimberly Allain emphasizes, "You're a master leader. This means mastery as a leader is your responsibility . . . living your values means you get to choose authentic vulnerability . . . all SBOs can start by beginning to trust. Even when everything around you says, there's nothing to trust."[12]

Values Support Basic Business Operations

I recently had a conversation with Stephane Schafeitel and was amazed. He said precisely what I teach clients, "Your *vision* describes where you are going. Your *mission* describes how you will get to where you are going. Your *values* describe how you behave during the journey."[13] I'm known for saying, "Business is an ongoing experiment," and it's relevant to this topic, as well. Experiment how values can be activated in every aspect of your business.

Most SBOs don't realize how significant applying values may have on every aspect of their business. Again, it's the *Art of Business.* Here's the truth: the subtlety and wisdom (applied knowledge) of values is your business's greatest differentiator. It changes everything.

When identified and appropriately applied, values: eliminate your competition and showcase you, provide appropriate strategies and tactics, generate strong marketing messages, alleviate stress and friction, support better decision making in real-time, and generate profit for your business while maintaining peace for yourself.

Business Relationships

Relationships are built upon values and expectations of values being upheld. Business agreements are expectations, which are premised on a common value of integrity. If you break trust, Kimberly Allain cautions, "You don't get back trust. Don't let your values be mere words posted on a website. Allow them to be experienced in your relationships."[14]

Being intrinsic, your values are freely expressed—either consciously and unconsciously—and are noticed by others. Susan White, LCSW, reminds us, "if you have an expectation of people reflecting your core values back to you, you may be disappointed."[15]

Testimonials also reveal your values to others. Dr. Ellema Neal uses testimonials to reflect upon how she is showing up, her customers' perceptions, and the potential of a particular brand.[16]

Chaplain Lisa Tuebel reminds SBOs to "stay true to oneself by staying in integrity. Every experience with people is an opportunity to be in integrity. If you falter, pardon yourself. The experience is priceless."[17]

Business Model

A foundational component of a business operation is developing an effective business model. SBOs have endless alternatives. Typically, SBOs choose a model they prefer. They don't think about whether or not it aligns with their values, their business's values, or their customers' values. Values are what we appreciate. Choosing an appreciated model and mode of delivery, by your marketplace, impacts your profitability. Begin by identifying what you appreciate, then what your marketplace appreciates.

When building or creating a business model or strategy, Dr. Ellema Neal stated, "I always start with values . . . If a business owner hasn't taken the time to really identify and get in touch with their own core values, both personally and professionally it actually shows in the way they do business and it shows in how they treat their employees, how they act with their competition, and how they treat their customers."[18]

Business Brand & Marketing

Susan White, LCSW shared, "My values are unique to me and my business – it's like free marketing . . . even though it isn't necessarily an immediate payoff, it will create profitability."[19]

Dr. Ellema Neal revealed, "Your core values are your seal . . . Business owners really don't create their brand, their customers and the community they serve do . . . Businesses can become more valuable when they measure themselves beyond profit: I've seen how this has increased market share and it's strengthened their brand."[20]

Business Priorities—The Struggle is Real

I've worked with thousands of business owners and leaders who all struggle with the same thing—not knowing and understanding their priorities. This creates a great deal of stress and overwhelm. When I tell people it is possible to have a profitable AND peaceful business, they look at me and sigh.

This naturally leads to the next question: "How do I know which of my priorities to focus on first?" This isn't a cookie-cutter answer. Many business activities have a *priority tag* attached to them on any given day. I wish I could wave a magic wand and give a standard answer, but it doesn't exist.

Unfortunately, the answer sought is personal, deeper, and requires an inquiry into personal values and core values. This discovery process will deliver the guiding answer of how to manage one's activities, as individually defined. Why am I suggesting personal values? Most small businesses don't have business values, so this will most likely default to personal values.

The solution isn't to work harder or faster, nor is it about recategorizing your to-do list. The solution is understanding your values and how they can support your performance, as well as your business's performance. "Values make decisions easy. Indecision and confusion is often the result of not knowing the relative importance of things you want."[21]

TIP: Since *reverence* is one of my core values, I work diligently to get all my deliverables out to others as soon as possible. Then, I'm free to work on my projects, which don't involve others needing something from me. I minimize my stress because I'm proactive and don't have as many mental distractions.

Business Culture

Again, we find culture as a hot business topic. I'm not referencing the focus on people and culture, we address this superlatively in Susan McCuistion's Chapter 3 and Dr. Shalini Nag's Chapter 4; rather, I'm referencing how values are foundational to culture.

I see phrases like, "Culture eats strategy for breakfast,"[22] by Peter F. Drucker, dubbed The Grandfather of Modern Business. Then I hear how it is twisted to mean something vastly different in this century and is used as a sexy sound bite or cliché. What's missing in the UN-Experts' clichés?[23] They aren't sharing how to go about creating a culture. An inquiry and strategy must be utilized to create and generate an intentional culture, which begins by identifying organizational values.

Tony Hseih, retired CEO of Zappos, is often credited for creating a great organizational culture. He explicitly shares the importance of values, "Your personal core values define who you are, and a company's core values ultimately define the company's character and brand. For individuals, character is destiny. For organizations, culture is destiny."[24]

Steve Jobs is one of the most revered contemporary CEOs. Jobs shared this about challenges and success, "The worst thing that could possibly happen as we get big and we get a little more influence in the world is if we change our core values and start letting it slide. I can't do that. I'd rather quit."[25]

Self-Leadership and Self-Management Rescue Small Business Owners

Internal conflict, stress, resistance, overwhelm, friction, agitation, etc., are all indicators of a misalignment(s). When you are experiencing these, it doesn't necessarily mean something is bad. These moments provide opportunities for you to make choices to better support your vision and truth.

As an SBO, self-leadership is creating a *vision*. Self-management is how you are going to get there (it's the *mission* part of this process).

Self-management is where your freedom is born. Paradoxically, it is born through discipline. If you are a parent, you're constantly trying to manage your child. Structure, boundaries, and discipline to deliver expectations are essential to succeeding. Structured success generates rewards—in business we call this profit, success, promotions, and growth. If you had more of this, would you be more interested in self-leading and self-managing?

REMEMBER: If you aren't leading your business, who is? Will there be a business to lead and manage?

Do You Value Your Business Enough to Dive into Your Values?

Do you ever find yourself disregarding what you promised? What about promises which pull you in different directions? Values keep you from drifting away from your goals and commitments.

"Open your arms to change but
don't let go of your values."[26]

— HH Dalai Lama

If you consciously choose to identify and act upon your core values, you will find a favorable impact for you and your business's performance. This helps you make better business decisions in real-time because of the clarity and the guidance values provide for many business activities. Values are the fabric weaving all business activities together through the beliefs, actions, and behaviors of all employees—internal and external.

Everyone has values. Typically, most SBOs haven't identified their values, nor how they are constantly exhibiting them. So how do you begin? By making better choices to support your peace and profitability.

Start Here: The Small Business Core Values Initial Inquiry™:

Pause: "Slow down to accelerate."[27]

Discern: Do I want to increase the value of my business?

Commitment: Am I willing to explore my values and three core values?

Activate: Am I willing to identify my business's three core values?

Amplify: Am I ready to infuse the business's values into every aspect of my business?

Typically, successful business owners focus on their personal development because they understand this is how success is best supported. You, and your business, need to leverage values. When you identify and apply your values, you experience peace because there is more alignment. Eventually, you find yourself living a more stress-free life and experience more joy. The value of your life and business appreciate. Doesn't this sound heavenly?

Susan White, LCSW, poses one last question: "Are core values deep, or do they run along the surface for others to see and experience?"[28] You have an opportunity to make a choice to support success. I encourage you to choose wisely—for your future self.

How Valuing Your Values Adds Value to Your Business Glossary:

Art of Business: Delicately paying attention to the little things. Knowing how to maneuver with skills and savvy. Mastery or finesse in business principles.

Authentic Self: Who you are versus who you are told you *should* be.

Business Model: A structure, form, or approach of how business is conducted.

Conscious: Being self-aware or mindful. Practicing awareness. Knowing.

Core Values: Your unwavering and foundational values. Reveal what you treasure most.

Discern: To sense or perceive. To be astute, mindful, or wise.

Intentional Culture: Created by people who utilize standardizing and aligning the organization's values (beliefs, attitudes, and behaviors.

Intrinsic: Naturally belonging. Something held within. Innate.

Misalignment: Out of alignment. Creating friction.

Priority Tag: A label assigned to a task or strategy according to its importance.

Science of Business: The nuts and bolts of business. What all businesses need to function.

Self-Leadership: The vision you hold for yourself or your business.

Self-Management: The necessary actions you take to actualize your vision. This requires structure, boundaries, accountability, and discipline to stay aligned with your vision or your business's vision.

Small Business: According to the Small Business Administration, small businesses are defined as having 1 – 499 employees.

Unconscious: A lack of awareness.

Values: Your most important beliefs, attitudes, and behaviors.

Meet Brilliant Practicing Expert™
Maggie Mongan:

Master Business Coach & Trainer | International Speaker
#1 Bestselling Author | Small Business Thought Leader

Raised in rural Wisconsin, #1 Bestselling Business Author, Maggie Mongan approaches business like many local farmers – practically, proactively, prayerfully, and always looking "Forward".

With over 30 years of leadership and management, Maggie serves Entrepreneurs and the Small Business Sector. She is a trusted guide, training clients on business's fresh perspectives to Simplify 21st century Small Business Success. Maggie is recognized as a Small Business Thought Leader. She enjoys melding her two worlds (Peace Minister and CEO) together to assist Small Business Owners to conduct business in a prosperous and peaceful manner. When she's on her downtime, you'll probably find her riding a Harley.

MAGGIE'S SPECIAL INVITATION FOR YOU:

Ready to begin exploring your values through *The Small Business Core Values Initial Inquiry*™?

Click: https://www.brilliantbreakthroughs.com/core-values/

BRILLIANT
BREAKTHROUGHS, INC
GUIDING & SIMPLIFYING YOUR BUSINESS BRILLIANCE

Business: Brilliant Breakthroughs, Inc.

Brilliant Breakthroughs, Inc. was established to help Small Business Owners learn how to optimize, not maximize, their business performance, and leadership.

Good news: there is a new way of conducting business! Maggie helps clients tame their business monster and build simplified business models for success by implementing her proprietary framework of *The 4 Performance Pillars for Small Business Success*™ (Profitability, People, Productivity, and Peace. Bottom line: Maggie swiftly helps Small Business Owners succeed by simplifying strategies and aligning actions to build their profitable and peaceful business.

Website: https://BrilliantBreakthroughs.com

Connect with Maggie on these social accounts:
LinkedIn: https://www.linkedin.com/in/MaggieMongan
Twitter: https://twitter.com/BrilliantBlogr
Facebook: https://www.facebook.com/BrilliantBreakthroughsInc/
YouTube: https://youtube.com/c/brilliantbreakthroughsinc Author
Author Profile: https://amazon.com/author/maggiemongan

Download Mobile App: BrilliantBizBook from your App Store.
It contains everything related to this Book Series and its Authors.

CONCLUSION

By now, I'm sure you noticed our team of *Brilliant Practicing Experts*™ is overflowing with best practices and unconventional approaches to help you succeed in 21st-century small business.

We hope you have built a plan (strategy) to take actions from whichever chapters will best serve you now. Each quarter, come back and find some more techniques to improve your business's performance.

REMEMBER: This book is dedicated to you. It is designed to make your job easier. The only thing I'd like to add is how to make this book work for you:

- Apply the strategies and techniques discussed here.
- Accept each author's invitations on their Author Page.
- Engage with the authors via their social media accounts.
- Download our Free Mobile App: BrilliantBizBook Why? Each author will have extra and ongoing support there for you through weekly podcasts, blogs, videos, and events.
- Go to amazon.com and let us know what you found useful and then let us know what you'd like to learn in our 2021 book.

START HERE: Get your ROI out of the book by following the above checklist and begin shining brightly! Then, go back to Volumes 1, 2, and 3 in our #1 Bestselling Business Book Series and begin applying its different and fresh perspectives. If you do this, you'll be ready for when we roll out Volume 5 (November 2021).

COLLECTIVE ENDNOTES

Introduction:

1. (George A. Santos, personal communication, July 7, 2017)

2. Abraham, M. (2015). *The entrepreneur's solution: the modern millionaire's path to more profit, fans & freedom.* New York: Morgan James Publishing.

3. Gary Vay-Ner-Chuk (@garyvee). Instagram photos and videos. (2017, July 7). Retrieved July 7, 2017, from https://www.instagram.com/garyvee/?hl=en

Chapter 1: The Financial Freedom Trail

1. Inspired Results, LLC, Silence, Rebeccah (2020, August 6). Personal Communication [Zoom Interview].

2. Hovich, Evelina (2020, August 8). Personal Communication [Zoom Interview].

3. Sparrow Solutions, Sparrow, Nancy (2020, August 5). Personal Communication [Zoom Interview].

4. BE. Design Your Life, Johnson, Angela (2020, August 7). Personal Communication [Zoom Interview].

5. Life Fuel, LLC, Potter, Katrina (2020, August 7). Personal Communication [Zoom Interview].

Chapter 2: Uplevel Your Business by Replacing Your Irreplaceable Employees: Move to Indispensable Key Talent for Ultimate Success

1. Amber Nusland – https://www.socialmediatoday.com/content/ indispensable-vs-irreplaceable, April 26, 2010

2. (Cindy Bacskai, personal communication, August 24, 2020.)

3. (Klint Kendrick, personal communication, August 22, 2020)

4. (Lou Adler, personal communication, August 26, 2020)

5. (Sharif Mansur, personal communication, August 27, 2020)

Chapter 3: The Hidden Cost of Doing Business

1. (Deborah Levine, personal communication, August 29, 2020)

2. (John Barth, personal communication, August 27, 2020)

3. (Amri Johnson, personal communication, August 28, 2020)

4. Britannica. (n.d.). Physiology. In *Britannica.com*. Retrieved August 30, 2020, from https://www.britannica.com/science/information-theory/Physiology

5. (Shrivallabh K, Co-founder – DimenZion3, personal communication, August 28, 2020)

6. Seppala, S. (2014, May 8). Connectedness & Health: The science of social connection. *The Center for Compassion and Altruism Research and Education.* http://ccare.stanford.edu/uncategorized/connectedness-health-the-science-of-social-connection-infographic/

7. Sissa Medialab, (2014, February 27). The pain of social exclusion: Physical pain brain circuits activated by "social pain." *Science Daily*. https://www.sciencedaily.com/releases/2014/02/140227101125.htm

8. Sue, D.W. (2011, February 27). How does oppression (microaggressions) affect perpetrators? *Psychology Today*. https://www.psychologytoday.com/us/blog/microaggressions-in-everyday-life/201102/how-does-oppression-microaggressions-affect

9. Marsh, J. (2012, March 29). Do mirror neurons give us empathy? *Greater Good Magazine.* https://greatergood.berkeley.edu/article/item/do_mirror_neurons_give_empathy

10. Smith, J.A. (2016, August 25). The science of the story. *Berkley Blog.* https://news.berkeley.edu/berkeley_blog/the-science-of-the-story/

11. Forbes Communication Council. (2020, March 2). 12 benefits of embracing vulnerability in leadership. *Forbes.* https://www.forbes.com/sites/forbescommunicationscouncil/2020/03/02/12-benefits-of-embracing-vulnerability-in-leadership/#3daef3962248

Chapter 4: Flip the Paradigm: Embrace the Human Approach to Boost Your Business

1. Nag, S. (2019). Culture Strategy. https://www.evidasolve.com/culture-strategy

2. Ismail, S., Malone, M. S., & Van Geest, Y. (2014). *Exponential Organizations.* New York, NY: Diversion Books.

3. Patel, S. (2015, August 06). 10 Examples of Companies with Fantastic Cultures. https://www.entrepreneur.com/article/249174

4. Montañez, R. (2019, December 10). The Best Companies for Corporate Culture In 2019. https://www.forbes.com/sites/rachelmontanez/2019/12/10/the-best-companies-for-corporate-culture-in-2019/#79950daa6dc3

5. (N. Wolfe, personal communication, May 6, 2020)

6. Lee, B. (2017). *Trust rules: How the world's best managers create great places to work*. Dublin, Ireland: Trust Lab.

7. Harter, J. (2020, April 17). Employee Engagement on the Rise in the U.S. https://news.gallup.com/poll/241649/employee-engagement-rise.aspx

8. Hayes, M., Chumney, F., Wright, C., & Buckingham, M. (2019). *The Global Study of Engagement Technical Report* (Tech.). https://www.adp.com/-/media/adp/resourcehub/pdf/adpri/adpri0102_2018_engagement_study_technical_report_release-ready.pdf

9. Solving employee disengagement. (2020, August 19). https://www.predictiveindex.com/learn/diagnose/resources/ebooks/solving-employee-disengagement/

10. Edmans, A. (2011). Does the stock market fully value intangibles? Employee satisfaction and equity prices. *Journal of Financial Economics, 101*(3), 621-640. doi:10.1016/j.jfineco.2011.03.021

11. (R. Racioppi, personal communication, May 26, 2020)

12. Parke, M., & Sherf, E. N. (2020, June 04). You Might Not Be Hearing Your Team's Best Ideas. https://hbr.org/2020/06/you-might-not-be-hearing-your-teams-best-ideas

13. Kirsh, A. Why Equality and Diversity Need to be SMB Priorities. https://www.salesforce.com/blog/2018/02/why-equality-and-diversity-need-to-be-priorities

14. McCuistion, S. (2018). Five Ways to bring Compassion to Your Organization. In *Brilliant Breakthroughs for the Small Business Owner: Fresh Perspectives on Profitability, People, Productivity, and Finding Peace in Your Business* (Vol. 2). USA: Brilliant Breakthroughs.

15. Barta, T., Kleiner, M., & Neumann, T. (2018, February 16). Is there a payoff from top-team diversity? Retrieved from https://www.mckinsey.com/business-functions/organization/our-insights/is-there-a-payoff-from-top-team-diversity#

16. (D. Pontefract, Personal Communication, May 28, 2020)

17. Hoffman, K. (2019). Digital Mindset Required: Preparing Small Business for a Quantum Leap. In *Brilliant Breakthroughs for the Small Business Owner: Fresh Perspectives on Profitability, People, Productivity, and Finding Peace in Your Business* (Vol. 3). USA: Brilliant Breakthroughs.

18. (K. Trigg, Personal Communication, May 13, 2020)

19. Ford, J., & Ford, L. (2009). *The four conversations: Daily communication that gets results*. San Francisco, CA: Berrett-Koehler.

20. Shore, J. (2016, February 23). Have You Mastered the 3 Rules of the Talk: Listen Ratio? https://jeffshore.com/2015/03/the-talk-listen-ratio-for-sales/

21. Robinson, A., & Schroeder, D. M. (2014). *The idea-driven organization: Unlocking the power in bottom-up ideas*. San Francisco: Berrett-Koehler.

22. (E. McNulty, personal communication, June 9, 2020)

23. Cooperrider, D. & Srivastva, S. (1987). Appreciative Inquiry in Organizational Life. Research in organizational change and development (Vol. 1).

24. (B. Wooditch, personal communication, May 27, 2020)

25. (D. Wagstaff, personal communication, May 7, 2020)

Chapter 5: Are Your Influencer Capabilities Being Overpowered by Imposter Syndrome?

1. https://www.merriam-webster.com/dictionary/imposter%20syndrome

2. (G. A. Santino Personal Communication July 23, 2020)

3. (A. Abrams Time.com Professional Journal June 20, 2018) https://time.com/5312483/how-to-deal-with-impostor-syndrome/

4. (G. A. Santino Personal Communication July 28, 2020)

5. (J. Rohn quote Written Correspondence Success. com January 2016) https://www.success.com/ jim-rohns-foundations-for-success/

6. (H. Ford quote Professional Journal by Erica Anderson May 31[st,] 2013) https://www.forbes.com/sites/ erikaandersen/2013/05/31/21-quotes-from-henry-ford-on-business-leadership-and-life/#5981d91293c5

7. https://www.merriam-webster.com/dictionary/influencer

8. (Aristotle's quote Psychology Today Professional Journal by Christopher Bergland Dec 28[th,] 2016) https://www. psychologytoday.com/us/blog/the-athletes-way/201612/ childhood-friendships-influence-both-fear-and-fearlessness

Chapter 6: Integrate for Well-Managed, Intentional Growth

1. Dobbs, R., Manyika, J., & Woetzel, J. (2018, February 9). *The four global forces breaking all the trends.* McKinsey & Company. https://www.mckinsey.com/business-functions/strategy-and-corporate-finance/our-insights/ the-four-global-forces-breaking-all-the-trends

2. Sebastian, F. (2020, July 29). *GDPR in the US: Requirements for US Companies.* Termly. https://termly.io/resources/articles/ gdpr-in-the-us/

3. Schwab, Klaus. (2016, January 14). "The Fourth Industrial Revolution: What It Means and How to Respond." *World Economic Forum*, World Economic Forum. www.weforum.org/

agenda/2016/01/the-fourth-industrial-revolution-what-it-means-and-how-to-respond/

4. NAICS Association. (2020, June). "US Business Firmographics – Company Size." *Counts by Company Size*. https://www.naics.com/business-lists/counts-by-company-size/

5. Studer, Q. (2017, October 4). *Ten Skills Every Entrepreneur And Small Business Owner Must Have*. Young Upstarts. https://www.youngupstarts.com/2017/10/04/ten-skills-every-entrepreneur-and-small-business-owner-must-have/

6. CFI Staff. (2020, June 14). *Knowledge Workers - Who They Are and What They Do*. Corporate Finance Institute. https://corporatefinanceinstitute.com/resources/knowledge/other/knowledge-workers/

7. Franklin, Benjamin. (1748, July 21). "Advice to a Young Tradesman." *Founders Online*, National Archives and Records Administration. https://founders.archives.gov/documents/Franklin/01-03-02-0130

8. Epstein, D. (2020, August 20). *20 Best Accounting Software for Small Business in 2020*. Financesonline.com. https://financesonline.com/top-5-accounting-software-small-business-2017/

9. SophyIn, J. (2017, April 4). *84 Percent of Small Businesses Rely on a Manual Process*. Small Business Trends. https://smallbiztrends.com/2017/04/manual-process.html

10. Nicastro, S. (2020, August 10). *25 Best Small-Business Apps*. NerdWallet. https://www.nerdwallet.com/article/small-business/20-apps-small-business-owners

11. de Bruyckere, P. (2016, December 18). *The "Law of the instrument"*. From experience to meaning...

https://theeconomyofmeaning.com/2016/12/18/
the-law-of-the-instrument/

12. Briercliffe, M. (2016, June 24). *The pros and cons of systems integration for small businesses*. The pros and cons of systems integration for small businesses - Hiscox Business Blog. https://www.hiscox.co.uk/business-blog/pros-cons-systems-integration-small-businesses

13. Adenle, C. (2020, August 21). *12 Reasons Why Employees Resist Change in the Workplace*. Catherine's Career Corner. https://catherinescareercorner.com/2011/07/26/12-reasons-why-employees-resist-change-in-the-workplace/

14. HelpSystems, I. B. M. (2020, August 10). *The Truth About Document Management Costs*. HelpSystems. https://www.helpsystems.com/blog/truth-about-document-management-costs

15. McCorry, K. J. (2009, September 16). *The Cost of Managing Paper: A Great Incentive to Go Paperless!* informIT. http://www.eco-officiency.com/downloads/InformIT_Cost_of_Managing_Paper.pdf

16. Turczynski, B. (2020, May 19). *2020 HR Statistics: Job Search, Hiring, Recruiting & Interviews*. zety. https://zety.com/blog/hr-statistics

17. Kislik, L., Dillon, K., Su, A. J., & Delizonna, L. (2018, November 4). *What to Do When You Realize You Made a Bad Hire*. Harvard Business Review. https://hbr.org/2018/08/what-to-do-when-you-realize-you-made-a-bad-hire

18. McKeown, G. (2014, November 2). *Hire Slow, Fire Fast*. Harvard Business Review. https://hbr.org/2014/03/hire-slow-fire-fast

Chapter 7: Building Confidence Along with a Successful Business - From the Ground Up

1. Dalai Lama, "With realization in one's potential and self-confidence in one's ability, one can build a better world." https://brainyquote.com/quotes/dalai_lama_387284#

2. "Confidence is a belief in oneself, the conviction that one has the ability to meet life's challenges and to succeed—and the willingness to act accordingly. Being confident requires a realistic sense of one's capabilities and feeling secure in that knowledge." https://psychologytoday.com/us/basics/confidence

3. Stewart Stafford, "Confidence is when you believe in yourself and your abilities, arrogance is when you think you are better than others and act accordingly." https://goodreads.com/quotes/9154100

4. (John Lee Dumas- Entrepreneurs on Fire. Personal communication. July 9, 2020)

5. Judi Holler- Profession Speaker- Fear Boss and CEO of Holla Productions. Online broadcasts, June 21, 2020.

6. (John Lee Dumas- Entrepreneurs on Fire. Personal communication, July 9, 2020)

7. Sinek, Simon. *Start with Why: How Great Leaders Inspire Everyone to Take Action*. Penguin Business, 2019.

Chapter 8: Uncover Your Cells' Stories, Discover Your Quantum Nature™ You are the Best Asset of Your Business

1. (A. Tucker, personal communication, Founder of business energetic and Author of *Undoubtedly Awesome.* August 2020)

2. (Dr. I. Perez, DDS, I-MD, Ph.D., personal communication, Co-founder of ISAMIZU, Quantum Health Consultant, Integrative Dentist, August 2020)

3. AMERICAN PSYCHOLOGICAL ASSOCIATION. (2017). *Stress in America: Coping with Change. Stress in America™ Survey* [Press release]. Retrieved from https://www.apa.org: https://www.apa.org/news/press/releases/stress/2016/coping-with-change.pdf

4. Baum, A., & Polsusnzy, D. (1999). Health Psychology: Mapping Biobehavioral Contributions to Health and illness., *50*, 137-163.

5. The Medical Expenditure Panel Survey (MEPS), 2008

6. Gaskin, D. J., & Richard, P. (2011). *Relieving Pain in America, A Blueprint for Transforming Prevention, Care, Education, and Research* [Press release]. Washington, D.C.: National Academies Press.

7. https://institute.jpmorganchase.com/institute/research/small-business/small-business-dashboard

8. (Dr. C. Burns, I-MD, Ph.D., personal communication, CEO of Carla Burns, Podcast Host of Claim Your Power. August 2020)

9. (M. Hayashi: personal communication, Ambassador and Global Director of Non-profit organization Emoto Peace Project. August 2020)

Chapter 9: How Valuing Your Values Adds Value to Your Business

1. "Change Is Good-But First, Know What Should Never Change." *Jim Collins - Articles - Change Is Good*, www.jimcollins.com/article_topics/articles/change-is-good.html.

2. Business Dictionary.com. Retrieved September 07, 2020, from Business Dictionary.com website: http://www.businessdictionary.com/definition/values.html

3. Covey, Stephen R. *The 7 Habits of Highly Effective People: Powerful Lessons in Personal Change Interactive Edition*. Mango Media, 2016.

4. Daum, Kevin. "18 Jon Stewart Quotes to Restore Your Sanity and Make You Laugh." *Inc.com*, Inc., 8 Sept. 2016, www.inc.com/kevin-daum/18-jon-stewart-quotes-to-restore-your-sanity-and-make-you-laugh.html

5. (Stephane & Shalee Schafeital, Personal communication, August 2, 2020)

6. Mongan, Maggie. "Core Values Support Your Business Growth." *Brilliant Breakthroughs, Inc.*, 30 May 2019, www.brilliantbreakthroughs.com/core-values-support-business-growth/.

7. Mongan, Maggie. "Core Values Support Your Business Growth." *Brilliant Breakthroughs, Inc.*, 30 May 2019, www.brilliantbreakthroughs.com/core-values-support-business-growth/

8. "What Are Core Values?" *National Parks Service*, U.S. Department of the Interior, www.nps.gov/training/uc/whcv.htm

9. "What Are Core Values?" *National Parks Service*, U.S. Department of the Interior, www.nps.gov/training/uc/whcv.htm

10. Markway, B. & Ampel, C. (2018) *The Self-Confidence Workbook*. Althea Press: Emeryville, CA. p. 28.

11. (Kimberly Allain, personal communication, July 26, 2020)

12. (Kimberly Allain, personal communication, July 26, 2020)

13. (Stephane & Schafeital, Personal communication, August 2, 2020)

14. (Kimberly Allain, personal communication, July 26, 2020)

15. (Susan White, personal communication, July 22, 2020)

16. (Dr. Ellema Neal, personal communication, July 26, 2020)

17. (Lisa Teubel, personal communication, July 24, 2020)

18. (Dr. Ellema Neal, personal communication, July 26, 2020)

19. (Susan White, personal communication, July 22, 2020)

20. (Dr. Ellema Neal, personal communication, July 26, 2020)

21. James, Matthew B. "Valuing Your Values." *Psychology Today*, Sussex Publishers, 15 June 2016, www.psychologytoday.com/us/blog/focus-forgiveness/201606/valuing-your-values

22. Hyken, Shep. "Drucker Said 'Culture Eats Strategy For Breakfast' And Enterprise Rent-A-Car Proves It." *Forbes*, Forbes Magazine, 7 Dec. 2015, www.forbes.com/sites/shephyken/2015/12/05/drucker-said-culture-eats-strategy-for-breakfast-and-enterprise-rent-a-car-proves-it/

23. Mongan, Maggie. *Brilliant Breakthroughs for the Small Business Owner: Fresh Perspectives on Profitability, People, Productivity, and Finding Peace in Your Business*. Brilliant Breakthroughs, Inc., 2017.

24. Hsieh, Tony. *Delivering Happiness A Path to Profits, Passion, and Purpose, p. 124,* Hachette UK, 2010.

25. Milian, Mark. "The Spiritual Side of Steve Jobs." *CNN*, Cable News Network, 7 Oct. 2011, www.cnn.com/2011/10/05/tech/innovation/steve-jobs-philosophy/index.html

26. Dalai Lama. (n.d.). AZQuotes.com Retrieved Sept 9, 2020, from AZQuotes.com Web site: https://2www.azquotes.com/quote/396750

27. Mongan, Maggie. "Slow Down to Accelerate Small Business Success." *Brilliant Breakthroughs, Inc.*, 16 Jan. 2017, www. brilliantbreakthroughs.com/slow-down-to-accelerate-success/

28. (Susan White, personal communication, July 22, 2020).

We would love to know what you gained
from this book.

We invite you to leave a review.

Thank You!